First published by
The Social Market Foundation,
December 2004

The Social Market Foundation
11 Tufton Street
London SW1P 3QB

Published with the kind support
of EDS and the IDeA

Designed by Paula Snell Design

Contents

Acknowledgements

This book was improved by a large number of people. Thank you to everyone who attended two research seminars at Templeton College, Oxford. The discussions there informed a great deal of the thinking that subsequently went into the commissioning of the essays that follow. It was especially valuable to share examples of innovation with the practitioners who attended. Thank you in particular to Keith Ruddle, for his help and hospitality.

A number of members of staff at the Social Market Foundation have been helpful in the course of the project but special thanks should go to Robin Harding who was the researcher at a crucial stage and whose diligence and intelligence was invaluable.

Finally, our thanks to Matthew Trimming formerly at EDS. Without his expertise, encouragement and financial help, this project would never have got off the ground and this book would never have seen the light of day.

Notes on contributors

David Bell is Her Majesty's Chief Inspector of Schools

Sir Michael Bichard is the Rector of the University of the Arts London

Steve Bundred is Chief Executive of the Audit Commission

Liam Byrne is Labour MP for Hodge Hill

Philip Collins is Director of the Social Market Foundation

James Crabtree is Visiting Fellow, Institute of Public Policy Research

Mary Harris is Head of the National Grid Transco Foundation

Niall Maclean is a Senior Fellow at the Social Market Foundation

Ann Rossiter is Deputy Director of the Social Market Foundation

Keith Ruddle is the Principal of Templeton College, Oxford

Gideon Skinner is Research Team Manager at MORI

David Varney is Chair of Business in the Community and Chief Executive of HM Revenue and Customs

Greg Wilkinson is a partner at Accenture and an Associate Fellow of the Social Market Foundation

Jonathan Williams is a Researcher at the Social Market Foundation

Introduction
Reinvention Again

Philip Collins and Liam Byrne

Executive Summary

Reinventing Government now more than a decade old –
offered ten principles for entrepreneurial government: steer not
row, empower communities, encourage competition, be driven
by mission, be oriented by results, satisfy the customer, earn
money don't spend it, prevent rather than cure, decentralise
and use market forces – are these principles still appropriate?

Ten Questions For A Social Market Checklist:

1. Are service outcomes clearly defined and measured?
2. Do citizens have access to appropriate information about
   service performance?
3. Do governance structures ensure an appropriate voice for
   citizens and communities?
4. Is it possible for new providers to emerge and establish
   themselves?
5. Is it possible for citizens to choose an alternative service
   provider?
6. Is it possible for service providers to fail?
7. Is there effective external national inspection and audit?
8. Is there a system in place for government intervention in
   response to consistently failing provision or poor standards?
9. Is funding related to demand rather than the preferences
   of providers?
10. Do providers have discretion over levels of pay (and reward)?

Public services in Britain have not yet been adequately reinvented – four themes are particularly crucial: choice, subsidiarity, information and leadership.

We must remember that the alternative to reform is not equal provision – the starting point is variation by social class – the welfare state is itself a site of capture by the middle class – this fact is the answer to the question of why reform is needed – access to health care, for example, varies significantly both by place and by social class – the least well-off receive a smaller share of health resources than the better-off even though they tend to require more – for example, lower social groups have a 20% lower operation rate for hip replacements despite having a 30% higher need.

Introduction

It is now a decade since Osborne and Gaebler published *Reinventing Government*. It very quickly achieved that rare accolade for a policy book in that politicians actually read it. Indeed, the then Governor of Arkansas, Bill Clinton, commented on the dust-jacket. It helped inspire the National Performance Review of the Clinton-Gore White House, and later, Labour's own Modernising Government programme. Osborne and Gaebler argued that a revolutionary restructuring of the public sector was under way; an 'American perestroika' in which market forces were gradually being introduced into monopolistic government enterprises.

Osborne and Gaebler set out a clear vision of entrepreneurial government. It fell neatly into ten guidelines.

The Ten Reinventing Government Principles

1. Steer, not row (or as Mario Cuomo put it, "it is not government's obligation to provide services, but to see that they're provided");

2. Empower communities to solve their own problems rather than simply deliver services;

3. Encourage competition rather than monopolies;

4. Be driven by missions, rather than rules;

5. Be results-oriented by funding outcomes rather than inputs;

6. Meet the needs of the customer, not the bureaucracy;

7. Concentrate on earning money rather than spending it;

8. Invest in preventing problems rather than curing crises;

9. Decentralize authority; and

10. Solve problems by influencing market forces rather than creating public programmes.

1 The scorecard is derived from Howard Davies's pamphlet for the Social Market Foundation in 1994, *Fighting Leviathan: Building Social Markets That Work*.

More than a decade later, many of these ideas are still deeply contentious in Britain. It seemed an opportune moment to ask two questions of this country: to what extent have the principles in *Reinventing Government* been established in practice and what set of principles would be appropriate for this updated text?

There are two sections to this book. In the first part, and later in this introduction, we try to establish that there is still a case to be answered. Public services in the UK, despite the very many examples of good practice, are still not as good as they should be. In the second section, the authors set out some principles for reform and some recommendations for policy.

Section One: Where Are We Now?

In the first chapter, Philip Collins evaluates public services in Britain today on the *Reinventing Government* principles. He presents a scorecard for public services and comes to the rather depressing conclusion that not nearly enough has changed[1]. There have been notable improvements in health but school choice remains heavily constrained by geography and capacity and no resilient split between purchaser and provider has developed. Local government services are still too dependent on central funding and accountability mechanisms and policing, which Howard Davies identified in 1994 as a prime candidate for reform, remains almost devoid of choice, governed in an incomprehensible way and still has a system of funding that prioritises all the wrong things.

Ten Questions For A Social Market Checklist:

1. Are service outcomes clearly defined and measured?

2. Do citizens have access to appropriate information about service performance?

3. Do governance structures ensure an appropriate voice for citizens and communities?

4. Is it possible for new providers to emerge and establish themselves?

5. Is it possible for citizens to choose an alternative service provider?

6. Is it possible for service providers to fail?

7. Is there effective external national inspection and audit?

8. Is there a system in place for government intervention in response to consistently failing provision or poor standards?

9. Is funding related to demand rather than the preferences of providers?

10. Do providers have discretion over levels of pay (and reward)?

This establishes that public services in this country have not been reinvented on the model of Osborne and Gaebler, but why should any such reform be necessary? The next chapter provides the answer.

Gideon Skinner, James Crabtree and the health team from McKinsey show that, even if we are satisfied with the current equity of provision, the expectations that the public have of public services will not be still. We are demanding more and more as time passes from services. It is worrying, as Gideon Skinner shows, that satisfaction seems to be declining as outcomes are, in fact, improving. The experience of rapidly improving private sector services may be part of the explanation, as the McKinsey team say has been the case in health care. People also now demand a level of convenience and choice from their public services that they are, as yet,

ill-equipped to provide. James Crabtree suggests that these
expectations may continue to run ahead of the capacity of
the services unless the public is in some way implicated in
the provision of the service.

Section Two: The Reinvention Principles
In the second part of the book, the principles on which
reform should be based are presented. There are four important
principles and, in so far as an edited collection like this has a
message, this is its message.

(i) Choice
The first principle is choice. More than any other message with
respect to public services, choice is apt to be misunderstood.
In Chapter Three, Niall Maclean, Ann Rossiter and Jonathan
Williams set out why the left ought to value choice systems.
They present the empirical data to show that well-designed
choice schemes can and do preserve equity at the same time as
raising efficiency. They show that choice can contribute to the
left's historic values, rather than detract from them. They also
begin to articulate a distinctively left-of-centre theory of choice
which develops the idea of supported choice or public service
agents. They are candid too about the limitations with, and
problems of, choice schemes. Their point is not that choice systems
always serve left-of-centre political aims but that they *can* do.

(ii) Subsidiarity
A choice system is one way of decentralising power. Another is
by the old social market principle of subsidiarity: power should
lie at the appropriate level. In their different ways, Chapters
Four and Five reveal the limitations of central government. In
Chapter Four, Mary Harris, Keith Ruddle and David Varney
reiterate the Osborne and Gaebler principle that it is the role
of government to steer not to row. This means, in practice, that
government needs to allow people the capacity to solve their
own problems, rather than attempting to solve them directly.
Harris, Ruddle and Varney also look at the many attempts that
have been made, during the last decade, to engage business
in the solutions to social policy problems. The exhortation to
business has had a mixed legacy thus far. One of the problems

is what the authors vividly call "the arthritic system". The regulation preventing new schools opening, for example, is severe. The outcome is a culture in which risk-taking is discouraged because failure attracts sanctions and success has no reward. The concentration of power in Britain is Sir Michael Bichard's main theme in Chapter Five. He suggests that the concentration of power at the centre, most notably in a civil service that he considers to be dysfunctional, is the principal reason why government has not been reinvented as it might have been.

(iii) Information, Audit And Inspection
The rise of audit and inspection has been a feature of public service reform since before the publication of *Reinventing Government*. The Education Reform Act of 1988 established an inspection regime which has hardly stopped growing ever since. There are two different views expressed in this book. Michael Bichard argues that we have become dulled by bureaucracy and that the National Audit Office and the Public Administration Committee have failed to sharpen accountability. Scrutiny has, in fact, reinforced traditional patterns of behaviour and the innovation and experiment that are so essential to Osborne and Gaebler has been systematically filtered out of the system. Poorly set targets, in other words, inhibit creativity. Rather than concentrate minds on results, target-setting has, too often, led to deferred decisions and perverse consequences. In Chapter Six, David Bell disagrees. He defends the role of inspection in policing national standards and in identifying failure though he does say that inspection itself needs to be reinvented. It needs to be more frequent, more forensic and less burdensome. If these objectives can be achieved, and David Bell is in no doubt that they can, then inspection and audit is a crucial part of the landscape of public services.

(iv) Leadership
The fourth principle is a *liet-motif* of all the others and a conspicuous absentee from *Reinventing Government:* effective leadership is vital. Keith Ruddle and Steve Bundred rectify this omission. In Chapter Seven Keith Ruddle says that public services cannot be led hierarchically as they involve far too many separate processes and far too many negotiations involving

thousands of actors. The fiat of a traditional leader, descending *de haut en bas*, is exactly the wrong approach. Unfortunately, the public services are not attracting and keeping the best operational leaders. Steve Bundred takes up the same theme in Chapter Eight, but with respect to political leadership. There is a tendency in public service reform to denigrate the place of politics. Bundred reminds us that public service provision and political conflict are necessary companions. Conflicts over scarce resources have to be settled by politicians who carry with them the legitimacy that comes from the ballot box. Bundred argues that effective political leadership is now more important than ever, but, unfortunately, much of it isn't good enough. He concludes that we need to pay far more attention than we do to leadership development. There is some evidence that it works, but very little evidence of real commitment to it within the political class.

In the final chapter, Greg Wilkinson draws some policy conclusions from the principles that have been adduced by the other authors. He also adds a plea for more work to follow on the way in which we measure value in public services. He argues that the painfully slow replication of good practice in the public sector, a frustration voiced by many of the other authors in the collection, will never be addressed until the incentives are sharpened by the extensive use of quasi-markets.

Finally, it is worth emphasising just *why* reform is still needed. There is a paradox about the welfare state: the most acute analysis has come from the academic left, in the work, amongst others, of Richard Titmuss, Brian Abel-Smith and Julian Le Grand[2]. Their thesis has been simple and damning: the welfare state has always been captured by the middle class and the poor, for whom the benefits were mainly intended, have received a poor deal. Yet it is the political left that most tenaciously defends a system that has failed to eradicate these inequalities. Any attempt at reform is knocked back with the claim that it will lead to disparities in provision. A brief tour of the health service will reveal that public services are already marked by great divergences in provision. This is not simply to say that there are inequalities in health between classes. These results may be as much to do with dietary habits as they have to do with the provision of public services. More simply, and more damagingly, the *welfare state itself* is the site of capture by the middle class.

2 Richard Titmuss, *Essays On The Welfare State*, Allen and Unwin, 1958, amongst other titles. Julian Le Grand, *The Strategy of Equality*, Allen and Unwin, 1982. As Brian Abel-Smith once wrote: "One of the main consequence of the development of the welfare state has been to provide free social services to the middle classes."

3 Human Fertilisation and
Embryo Authority, 29 August
2002.

The rest of this book is a prospectus for reform and so it is vital to be clear about our starting point. Whatever may be the other virtues of monopoly public services, equal provision is unquestionably not amongst them. Therefore, it is at least open to question why one would wish to defend monopoly supply so vigorously, from the principle of equity. This is the answer to the question often posed by opponents of further change: *why* we do need reform? The answer is this: the current provision is unfair. It varies enormously by locale and poor areas always do worse than rich areas. If this variation were the spontaneous outcome of the will of the people it would not be alarming. But of course it is no such thing. The point of reform is to secure the original objectives of the welfare state. If we believe, reasonably enough, that properly organised public provision *could* make the world fairer (if not exactly fair) then we would have to conclude in all honesty that we have not devised it yet.

Variation By Place

It is important to distinguish between *health* and the outcomes of the health service. There is a danger of blaming health professionals for the fact that people sometimes get ill. Health inequalities are not wholly attributable to variations in performance. However, it is often said that access to health care goods is allocated by a postcode lottery. There is a good deal of truth in this cliché, as the examples below illustrate:

Geographical Variations In Healthcare Provision

- Inner-city areas are likely to have fewer GPs and poorer facilities: Oxfordshire has twice as many GPs per head of population as Gateshead and twice the level of funding

- There are large and inexplicable variations in almost all indicators of hospital performance. Different regions, for example, have very big differences between the highest and the lowest rates of death within 30 days of surgery after non-emergency admissions

- Success rates for fertility treatments are increasing but there is wide variation between the least and most successful clinics[3]

- Healthcare for people with diabetes varies greatly, depending on where they live. Some parts of Britain have only one third of the number of hospital doctors specialising in diabetes compared to other regions[4]

- The survey of consultant staffing levels in diabetes showed that in South Yorkshire there is one consultant per 55,000 whereas in Essex there is only one per 179,000 people

- Expenditure on patients with Alzheimer's varies between £91 and £2.[5]

4 Diabetes UK, Diabetes: It's Bloody Serious campaign.

5 Alzheimer's Society, submission to Health Select Committee, 2002.

If these geographical variations were the outcome of local policy decisions then there would be nothing wrong with them. But they are not. They are the unchosen outcome of a system that purports to be comprehensive. There will always be some variation between regions, reflecting the different policies that are taken by hospital managers, for example. But variations on this scale surely give the lie to the idea that public service provision, as it is currently constituted, is even tending towards egalitarian outcomes. It palpably is not. The most alarming fact is that provision is tending to reproduce, rather than challenge, the existing state of inequality according to social class.

Variation By Class

The postcode lottery, of course, conceals a deeper and more troubling distinction: between the well-off and the not very well-off. It is not simply the case that there are geographical variations in provision and that access to those variable services is equal. It is worse than that. Not only do the least well off receive the worst services, they also suffer a shortfall in access to those services that are provided. In The *Strategy of Equality* Julian Le Grand demonstrated that spending on health care was weighted towards the better-off. He showed that, in hospitals, community health, GPs, dental services, pharmaceuticals and ophthalmic services, expenditure per ill person grew as we ascended the social scale from class V to class I. Professionals, employers and managers received over 40% more than semi-skilled and unskilled manual workers. Doctors spent 50% more time on consultations with patients from social class I than they did with patients from social class V. There are a number of possible reasons for this: the middle classes may be better informed about what is available, better able to obtain it and more inclined to

6 British Journal of Cancer, March 2004.

7 Dixon, Anna, Le Grand, Julian, Henderson, John, Murray, Richard, and Poteliakhoff, Emmi (2003), 'Is the NHS equitable? A review of the evidence', *LSE Health and Social Care Discussion Paper Number 11*, London.

do so. They may be more aware of the benefits and it costs them less to use a free service; less travelling time, less waiting time through use of appointments, no loss of pay for being there.

These problems remain. The gap in survival rates from the 20 most common cancers grew between 1986 and 1999 in each five-year period studied. Disparities between the most and least deprived groups (according to ward of residence) was as high as 17.2% for men from cancer of the larynx, and had increased in 12 out of 16 cancers for men, and 9 out of 17 for women. The overall pattern of survival rates was found to offer strong evidence of a widening deprivation gap in cancer survival[6]. A recent study by the Commission for Health Improvement of variations in patient experience, based on an extensive survey of 370,000 patients using the services of 480 NHS organisations across England, found that up to 16% of the overall variation in patient experience observed could be accounted for by age, gender, education status, ethnic origin, trust type, method of admission, place of residence, and local deprivation. Those in more deprived areas had more negative experience of Primary Care Trusts, particularly in the fields of access, information and relationships.

Access For The Poor

There is a lot of evidence that higher socio-economic groups are more likely to have elected for health care while lower socio-economic groups are more likely to come into contact for the first time on an emergency basis. There are hundreds of examples of unequal access. In a review of the literature called "Is the NHS equitable?[7] Anna Dixon, Julian Le Grand, John Henderson, Richard Murray and Emmi Poteliakhoff present the evidence that lower income, less educated and unemployed groups did not use health services as much relative to their need as their richer, better educated peers. There is good evidence to this effect in cardiac, diagnostic and surgical care, elective procedures for hernia, gallstones, tonsillitis, hip replacements, and grommets, in-patient oral surgery, immunisation for diphtheria, pertussis, measles, mumps and rubella, diabetes clinics and diabetes reviews.

A national survey conducted in 2002 found that individuals who are unemployed, or have lower income or educational qualifications, are less likely to have outpatient, day case and in-patient treatment in the NHS – despite the fact that these groups consistently have a greater need for health services. Moreover, it is not simply because worse-off individuals are failing to present themselves to the health services in due time. Several studies have found that, in one way or another, the worse-off are being failed *within* the system. Goddard and Smith set out to survey the 'concordance between expressed need for possible surgical intervention [consulting a General Practitioner] and subsequent surgical intervention'. They found that marked socio-economic differences in consultation rates for primary care were not reflected in operation rates for all conditions'. In other words, worse-off individuals would present themselves to their GP, but would not then receive the secondary care they required. Across a number of conditions, members of the most deprived population were the most likely to consult with a GP, but they were the least likely to receive surgery. Individuals on lower incomes are more likely to consult their GP but are less likely to receive *all* forms of secondary care[8]. There is a similar tale in elective surgery. A study of the North East Thames Regional Health Authority showed that, for hernias, gallstones and osteoarthritis, members of the most deprived population were the most likely to consult a GP but were the least likely to receive surgery.

8 Having examined data from the national Health Survey for England through 1988 to 2000, along with a rich set of self-reported and objective data on individual health status, Morris, Sutton and Gravelle. This finding was supported by the work of O'Donnell et al.

Access To Health Care Goods By Social Class

- Lower social groups have a 20% lower operation rate for hip replacements, despite having around 30% higher need for them (where need is reported by them to their GP)

- Intervention rates for Coronary Artery Bypass Graft (CABG) or angiography following heart attack were 30% lower in the lowest socio-economic group than in the highest socio-economic group

- CABG and anglioplasty rates were 40% higher for the 'affluent achievers' than they were for the 'have nots'

- While death rates from coronary heart disease improved for everyone between 1976 and 1993 the ratio between deaths in manual and non-manual classes increased by 30%

9 Iona Heath, Royal College
of General Practitioners, 2003.

- A one point increase in the Carstairs 7-level index of deprivation is associated with a 3.4% decrease in the length of GP consultation. A 50% increase in consultation length is associated with a 32% increase in recognition of psychological distress

- The most common reason cited for not attending out of hours emergency care was lack of a car

- Non-attendance for a health check among 2678 invited patients is higher (27%) amongst patients who had access to a car against those who didn't (16%)

- 33% of manual workers indicate that taking time off work hindered their access to a GP, compared with 13% of non-manual workers

- Yorkshire Regional Health Authority found that social classes IV and V have 10 per cent fewer preventive consultations than social classes I and II.

Across a disparate and wide range of diseases, studies suggest that lower socio-economic groups tend to present with more advanced and with more severe diseases. For example, in spite of higher rates of ischaemic heart disease among people of South Asian origin in the United Kingdom, this group present to cardiology services at a later stage of disease when compared with their European counterparts. Yet a questionnaire survey found that people of South Asian origin reported a greater likelihood of seeking immediate care for angina symptoms than people of European origin, suggesting the delays in obtaining specialist care are due to differences in the care received rather than differences in illness behaviour[9].

This case has, strangely, not been very well-made. Too often the political left has found itself defending imperfect structures. There is no need to do so. Of course, the welfare state was an enormous improvement on the pattern of provision it replaced. The case that needs to be made is for reform not destruction. The first step is to concede that it has been a disappointment by its own lights. Then we need to search for policy mechanisms that can genuinely serve those objectives, ruling out nothing on ideological grounds. Some of those levers are the subjects of the chapters that follow in the rest of this book.

Chapter One
The Reinventing
Government Scorecard

Philip Collins

Executive Summary

Osborne and Gaebler endorsed government that steered rather than rowed which meant an embrace of markets and a reform of management – successive governments in the UK have followed these two precepts – they were supplemented by the four principles from the Office of Public Services Reform: national standards, devolution, flexibility and choice – extra money has increased the need for reform and there has been a lot of managerial change but not a great deal of it market-led.

In education, the system is organised around parental choice in which money follows the pupil, backed by a strong central inspection regime – in theory popular schools can expand, poor schools can close and new schools can open – this has meant private contractors running schools – an alternative is that poor schools can become federated with good schools – in practice school choice remains heavily constrained by geography and capacity – very little in the way of a split between purchaser and provider has developed in LEAs which means, for example, that no market in school management has emerged – the virtues of competition are thus missing and they have not been replaced by enough innovation in the form of different types of institution.

In health, the purchaser-provider split has been retained with the purchaser refashioned as a PCT – the structure of accountability has been overhauled with a range of new inspectorates and a star system – a tariff system will create a quasi-market for hospital trusts – there have also been salutary supply side changes such as independent Diagnostic Treatment Centres and the concordat with the private sector – Private Finance Initiative is now 25% of NHS capital expenditure but all the other reforms do not, as yet, extend very far into the system.

In policing, a stronger targets and audit regime has been introduced and an attempt to standardise police procedures through the Crime and Disorder Partnerships and the National Intelligence Model – this does not amount to much reform: there is little choice, funding bears no relation to performance or local priorities and corporate governance is incomprehensible – neither has a split between purchaser and provider been introduced apart from some limited experiments with wardens and security – funding is very much still wedded to inputs and very few secondary markets have emerged.

In local government, councils, which employ more people than the NHS, have seen some reforms to the model of democratic accountability: mayors and the leader-plus-cabinet system – the Comprehensive Performance Assessment (CPA) brings together a number of performance assessments – the duty to put services out to competitive tender has been replaced by Best Value – while there are some market pressures local authorities are still poor at controlling process costs and asset management. In practice funding does not reinforce accountability as only 26% comes from council tax – the process of improvement is very slow – the government has responded by creating Local Strategic Partnerships and a glut of other community-level initiatives – however this has not been accompanied, as it might and should have been, with deregulation and greater freedom for councils, especially those which score an excellent rating in the CPA.

Osborne and Gaebler, Thatcher and Major

The question of how government can be more effective is never far behind the argument about the role that government should play. Osborne and Gaebler, unusual for thinkers from the left, were not very sanguine about the prospect of government attaining its ends if it actually undertook direct execution of the job itself. They endorsed instead a conception of a government that 'steered' rather than 'rowed'. There were two ideas at the heart of *Reinventing Government*: an embrace of market mechanisms and a commitment to overhauling the techniques of public sector management. Osborne and Gaebler allowed much greater latitude for the invisible hand of competition, contestability and choice. They also sought to strengthen the rather more visible hand[1] of public sector management by importing many of the commercial techniques popularised by Tom Peters in *In Search of Excellence* including decentralisation, deregulation, mission statements and performance measurement.

Osborne and Gaebler captured the essence of many techniques then growing in currency[2] while providing something of a recipe book for public sector reformers for the future. Practically every major reform of public services over the last twenty-odd years has been driven by an attempt to create more of a market or to raise the levels and standards of management within the public sector. In the UK, the emphasis has veered between these two foundations. Much (though not all) of the reform of the Thatcher era was about increasing competition and choice through purchaser/provider splits, competitive tendering, more open enrolment in schools and tenant ballots in housing. Much (though not all) of the Major government's reform efforts were focused on making services more managerial, with a particular emphasis on accountability through league tables and increasing amounts of inspection and audit[3].

Perhaps the most important precept suggested by Osborne and Gaebler was that government ought to steer rather than row. This means directing the provision of services rather than necessarily providing them. No providers should be ruled out on ideological grounds.

Money, markets and management

The Prime Minister enunciated four principles for public service reform in 2001[4]. These were codified in the 2002 *Principles Into Practice* and confirmed (to an extent) by the H. M. Treasury publication *Public Services: Meeting the Productivity Challenge*[5]. The burden of both is that the user should come first:

1 This contract between Adam Smith's invisible hand of the market and the 'visible hand' of managers is owed to Alfred Chandler (1977), *The Visible Hand: The Managerial Revolution in American Business* (Cambridge, MA: Harvard University Press, Belknap).

2 For example, many of the market-based reforms implemented by the Thatcher administration, such as contracting out, had been developed in Conservative councils and publications during the late 1970s and early 1980s.

3 For this analysis I owe Greg Wilkinson.

4 Tony Blair, speech at the Royal Free Hospital, London, 16th July 2001.

5 H. M. Treasury, April 2003.

6 The Treasury re-expressed these as outcomes, devolved responsibility for the delivery of public services subject to effective governance structures, stronger governance sustained by improved performance information and better incentives for service providers to meet users' needs.

7 Following the 2002 Spending Review, Labour committed to raising public sector spending by some £125 billion over 3 years – a 5.25% real annual increase. Education spending will have increased by more than £1,000 per pupil in real terms by 2006. Health spending will have increased by 48% in real terms between 2001 and 2008.

8 And even in the private sector, that capacity is under severe pressure. Inflation in public sector construction costs is around 11%.

1. National standards that 'really matter to the public'

2. Devolution and delegation to give local leaders 'the opportunity to design and develop services around the needs of local people'

3. Flexibility and incentives for public service organisations to challenge 'restrictive practices'

4. Expanding choice to ensure that people had a choice about 'the kind of service they can have'[6].

The Labour governments since 1997 have addressed *both* management and markets - backed by a lot of money[7]. The stakes were set very high by the Prime Minister when he said that "if the Right is able to claim through our inability to reform these [public] institutions, or promote choice for the individual citizen, that public services are inherently flawed, we will see support for them wither and the clamour for private provision increase". Thus, the extra money *increases* the necessity for reform rather than reduces it. In practice, much of Labour's managerial reforms have been system-level redesigns (such as the restructuring of the health service) with enormous energy invested in the creation of an entire universe of accountability structures – plans, targets and inspectorates.

The second front – boosting markets - has been rather slower to open although the huge increase in public sector construction has forced the sourcing of private capacity.[8] Choice too has proved a difficult concept. With the notable exception of healthcare (and even here, the scale is limited), choice has more often meant choice about the mode of service delivery than a meaningful selection between competing providers proffering differentiated value propositions.

Perhaps the most important precept suggested by Osborne and Gaebler was that government ought to steer rather than row.

Connecting HMG and Reinventing Government

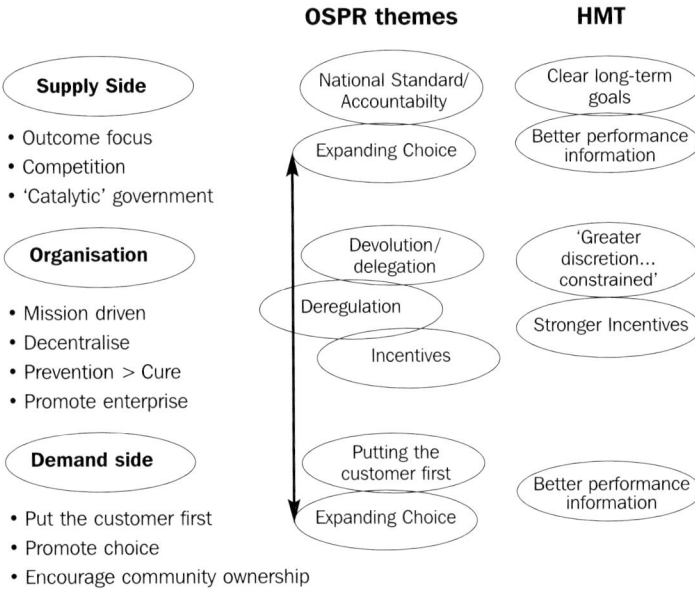

OSPR themes · HMT

9 Private interview.

10 The scorecard idea itself borrows heavily from Howard Davies's 1992 pamphlet for the SMF, cited above.

11 Glennerster, Howard (1997), *Paying for Welfare – Towards 2000,* Hemel Hempstead.

Supply Side

- Outcome focus
- Competition
- 'Catalytic' government

Organisation

- Mission driven
- Decentralise
- Prevention > Cure
- Promote enterprise

Demand side

- Put the customer first
- Promote choice
- Encourage community ownership

National Standard/ Accountabilty — Clear long-term goals

Expanding Choice — Better performance information

Devolution/ delegation — 'Greater discretion... constrained'

Deregulation — Stronger Incentives

Incentives

Putting the customer first — Better performance information

Expanding Choice

So, some ten years after *Reinventing Government,* we might be, as one former senior Treasury official put it, 'talking the right language'[9], but what has actually happened? Have public services been reinvented? This essay is a contribution to answering that question. I look in some detail at Education, Health, Policing and Local Government services and then conclude by judging the current state of public services on criteria which have been derived from Osborne and Gaebler. This is the public services scorecard[10].

Education: markets and management in theory

The policy framework which Labour inherited – national standards and inspectors, local freedom to manage, a degree of choice for citizens and funding that follows pupils – had many strengths, and indeed has been credited with driving the 'long boom' in UK education performance at a time (1995-2000) when 'schools gained little by way of extra resources'[11]. Wisely, the government has retained and augmented the key features. Literacy and numeracy hours have supplemented the National

Curriculum. Parental choice was confirmed by the 1998 School Standards & Framework Act and by the 2002 Education Act which says that Local Education Authorities must grant parental preference unless certain conditions are met. Parents have the right to appeal to an independent panel if their choice is not granted. To ensure that demand patterns create consequences for school managers, funding follows the pupil. So, although cash is passed to schools via LEAs in two blocks - Education Standard Spending and the Standards Fund - LEA discretion over education funding has been reduced. Direct delegation of funding to schools has risen from 79% of the budget in 1997-98 to 86.5% in 2001-02.

To toughen market forces, popular, successful schools can now expand by publishing proposals which a local School Organisation Committee (SOC) and School Adjudicators must approve, unless there is evidence that expansion will have a damaging effect on standards overall in the area. Nor do schools any longer need the extraordinary facility of a Statutory Instrument to change their capacity targets. Furthermore, government now helps fund approved expansion with a £500,000 grant (£400,000 where the school has no 6th form). If a LEA does not approve the expansion but the government chooses to provide funding, the school can then reclaim the money from the LEA budget.

Alternatively a community can open new schools – with new school managers - to increase local choice and competition. Under the Education (Additional Secondary School Proposals) Regulations 2003, an LEA must invite other interested parties - parents, community groups, private and charitable companies, faith communities - to bring forward proposals before it publishes its own proposals for a new school, creating the potential for an open competition between models of supply. The Secretary of State has the final say on which proposal should be successful.

Where schools are failing to achieve the national standards set for them they are in theory easier to close or remove from the market. Schools are inspected by Ofsted every six years[12], and if found to have serious weaknesses the school has a short time to save itself or face Special Measures, which involves a detailed rescue plan, and possibly external intervention. Since the 1998 School Standards & Framework Act, the Education Secretary can require an external partner to be brought in to a

failing LEA or school. This can and has meant private
contractors actually running public schools.

Alternatively, under the 2002 Education Act, two or more
maintained schools can be federated under a single governing
body in a variety of combinations. In Peterborough, for example,
the LEA's own monitoring led it to federate two schools before
Ofsted determined its own measures. A good school provided
governing body, financial control (and so effectively all decision
making power) but the senior management team of the poorly
performing school remained in post with the head of the good
school acting as a consultant.

13 Interestingly, the
Technology College Trust is
beginning to form national
networks in which school
leaders are able to access
some of the benefits of
'industrial organisation' such
as access to specialist R&D,
grouped procurement and
sourcing and so on.

Education: markets and management in practice

Despite these reforms, two fundamental challenges remain.
The first is that choice and competition are in reality highly
constrained by geography and the capacity of the system.
LEAs aim to provide a school place for each child but unless
there is excess capacity, every school is certain to fill all its places
and the funding formula rules out price competition. While
there are, in theory, new opportunities for alternative schools to
spring up, the initiative still lies with an LEA. While popular
schools *can* expand, Government provides only 25% of the typical cost of expanding facilities. Unsurprisingly, just 3 proposals
to expand under the new arrangements have been submitted.

The second problem is the lack of an effective purchaser-
provider split in LEAs in which the organisation of asset ownership severely constrains the action of market forces. Choice
and competition have not, therefore, been extended into the
discrete field of school management nor to any real extent into
the markets for asset management and back-office and support
services. Although we know very well that good school
management has a huge bearing on the performance of a
school, a significant market in school management services,
in which governing bodies (or indeed LEAs) are allowed to
appoint – or exercise a choice over - the management team, has
not emerged. Heads and managers remain the employees of the
LEA or school, cut off from the benefits of combination into
nation-wide enterprises[13] operating in competition with each
other. While many parts of the public economy have benefited
from a separation of assets from operations and the reorganisation

14 *Evaluation of new ways of working in local education authorities*, Volume 1; Main report for the DfES, Indepen and Bannock Consulting, May 2003.

15 Which let us not forget encompasses everything from what schools can pay teachers (school teachers pay is largely statutory, so it would be illegal to vary from the national spine), who can be deployed in the classroom (teachers are still the only people allowed to work independently in the classroom), and how schools can use school assets.

of asset management (either on a mutual or for-profit basis) on a larger and more economic scale, the education sector has not. Some grouped Private Finance Initiative (PFI) schemes and projects like Building for the Future have begun to reveal the potential of a different approach but they are isolated examples. Indeed there is fairly widespread hostility to outsourcing anything amongst LEAs[14].

The virtues of competition have thus gone missing and choice remains thinly limited to selecting providers in a monochrome public supply market. To add diversity to the supply-side, the government has encouraged schools to specialise and has now legislated to make it easier for schools to develop new models of school management. The Extended Schools pilots are exploring how multiple public services can be delivered from a single school site. City Academies have considerable freedom from standard school operating conditions – including the Teachers Pay and Conditions of Service Act, and the 'power to innovate' which gives the DfES the power to permit schools or LEAs to derogate from educational legislation if profitable innovation can thereby follow.

Here again, though the practice still falls short. Only 12 of more than 2,000 comprehensive schools are Academies. The school regulations mean that detailed permission is required for schools to do almost everything: from altering the length of the school day, exempting children from national curriculum tests (one for KS2 and one for KS3) or giving everyone free school meals[15]. Quite why schools require such detailed prescription when, for example, a general framework is considered to be sufficient for financial markets, is not at all clear.

While popular schools can expand, Government provides only 25% of the typical cost of expanding facilities. Unsurprisingly, just 3 proposals to expand under the new arrangements have been submitted.

Health: markets and management in theory

The basic 'purchaser-provider' principle has been retained from the Conservatives' internal market. Funding still follows the patient, but the 'purchaser' has been re-fashioned as Primary Care Trusts (PCTs) which have replaced the previous system of GP fund-holders. The framework of accountability in which the health service operates has been comprehensively over-hauled. Hospitals have National Service Frameworks which specify the nature and level of services patients are entitled to, a 'star system' in which they are rated one to three and several acronym-heavy sets of inspectors[16].

Although important innovations such as NHS Walk-in Centres and NHS Direct provide choice in primary care, health choice is principally delivered through the retained purchaser-provider split between GPs and NHS health trusts. In this system, doctors help patients choose a hospital and the funding then follows the patient. Thus, 75% of health funds are now disbursed by regionally organised Strategic Health Authorities to the Primary Care Trusts according to a complex capitation formula[17]. Primary Care Trusts fund the GPs and purchase hospital and other care for their patients, through block payments for capacity at NHS Trusts.

This semi-autonomy for PCTs introduces an element of competition in the acute care market between hospital trusts. Although today payments are made for theoretical capacity regardless of the volume actually delivered, this will soon change to a system where purchasing trusts pay hospitals for treatments actually delivered at a standard national tariff, allowing (in theory) efficient hospitals to make a profit on certain types of procedures, recycling the money into renewed investment to offer better services thereby boosting the chances of attracting more patients.

There have also been some reforms to the supply side which are strengthening competition in markets for certain procedures. Independent Diagnostic and Treatment Centres (DTCs)[18], the huge increase in minor surgery offered by GP's PCT facilities, and the Concordat with the Independent Healthcare Association, all boost competition. In 2002 patients waiting more than six months for a heart operation were permitted to insist on an alternate provider. This included,

16 Including, but not limited to: the Audit Commission, which works on value for money; the Commission for Health Improvement, which reviews clinical governance and inspects serious failures; the National Care Standards Commission, responsible for non-NHS doctors, hospitals and care homes; Health Authority Inspection Units, inspecting local establish-ments; the National Institute for Clinical Excellence, which spreads best practice; and the Health and Safety Executive, responsible for the health of NHS workers, but able to contribute to assessment of the health of patients as well. This will be simplified when the Commission for Healthcare Audit and Inspection takes over from the Commission for Health Improvement in 2004, absorbing the related work of the Audit Commission, and taking on responsibility for the star-rating of hospitals.

17 Based on the age of the target population, their state of health, and regional variations in cost (a similar model to local council grants).

18 Intended to complement hospitals by providing high volumes of elective treatment (cataract operations etc.) in specialised areas, several DTCs have already been built within the NHS and the government is proposing trials in the independent sector on five-year contracts to provide a fixed level of capacity.

19 Although three national pay spines are being introduced (for doctors, nurses, and other directly employed staff), so as to pay for the work being done, and not by the job title.

20 So debt will not carry an explicit government guarantee.

under the NHS Concordat, the private sector, or providers abroad. Within the next few years the plan is that patients will be referred and offered a choice of appointment times and of providers.

Two further 'reinventions' bear a mention. There is, first, the successful 'unbundling' of many operational functions and the emergence of secondary markets to serve these needs on a sensible, more economic scale. Driven in large part by PFI – which now accounts for 25% of NHS capital expenditure – a small but increasing proportion of assets and support functions, from patient management systems to catering to back-up energy generators, are provided by the market acting on a national (and sometimes global) scale.

Second, the freedom of local managers to manage has been extended. For most hospitals, operating constraints are very tight. The 1990 NHS and Community Care Act sets out financial policies including the obligation to break even, and although NHS Trusts can in theory borrow and form trading companies, in practice hospitals face restrictions on their use of surplus funds. National Service Frameworks set out standard procedures, and national pay agreements (which cannot be varied according to the local labour markets) set out standards for pay and rations[19]. All hospitals however now benefit from a degree of labour market deregulation that for example allows nurses to order tests and administer an IV. More fundamentally, NHS Foundation Trusts will be able to retain operating surpluses and the proceeds from asset disposals. Like NHS Trusts, Foundation Trusts will be able to borrow but uniquely, the Secretary of State will not be able to restrict borrowing[20]. With no power to pay dividends, Foundation Hospitals are free to focus exclusively on reinvesting spare cash into services.

Health: markets and management in practice
Despite all these welcome structural changes, the real choice on offer for patients is actually very limited. The same applies to the use of private sector capacity: in the winter of 2000/01 the NHS paid for 10,527 private sector operations out of a total of 6.5 million operations. Block contracts between PCTs and NHS Trusts severely constrain real competition in the

acute care market and the number of contracts to be issued for DTCs is limited, with both capacity and prices centrally planned, constraining competitive incentives. And, whereas NHS Trusts are somewhat exposed to patient pressure, GPs are not. PCTs are effectively unelected local monopolies governed by boards appointed by the Secretary of State. A community, therefore, relies rather a lot on the intolerance of under-performance of busy regulators far away.

Policing: markets and management in theory
In 1992, Sir Howard Davies wrote; 'the police…show all the characteristics of a badly designed system, one ripe for fundamental reform'[21]. It is hard to avoid the same conclusion a decade on. The sweep of Labour's reforms has affected the police much less than other parts of the public sector.

The inherited accountability structure has been augmented. A targets regime and a stronger audit framework have been introduced, the cornerstone of which is the 'Best Value' regime (similar to that governing local councils) and which includes by way of Statutory Order, the edict that police forces must set reduction targets for vehicle crime, domestic burglary and, in five large metropolitan forces, robbery[22]. Overall, some 32 Best Value Performance Indicators, including measures of recorded crime, have been drawn up and are monitored across all forces.

The HM Inspectorate of Constabulary manages the system. It inspects police forces and Basic Command Units, and carries out thematic inspections - on gun crime for example – together with the Police Standards Unit added by the Police Reform Act 2002 to the Home Office and charged with measuring and comparing Basic Command Unit (BCU) performance and identifying and disseminating best practice. This to complement some thirteen major pots of money handed out to support centrally determined priorities[23].

The final piece of the accountability jigsaw is the government's attempt to standardise approaches to policing, just as it has in teaching and health. Police procedure, is of course, quite tightly regulated by the Police and Criminal Evidence Act 1984 but Labour has sought to extend standardisation from operational procedure to strategic management with two measures:

21 Howard Davies, op.cit.

22 This is in support of national targets for a cut in vehicle crime of 30% by 2004, a cut in domestic burglary of 25% by 2005 and a 14% cut in big city robberies by 2005.

23 These include In 2003/04: ring-fenced grants to local authorities for a Crime Fighting Fund (£250m), a Rural Policing Fund (£26m), the Police Negotiating Board (£36m), a DNA database (not given), Basic Command Units (£47m), Community Support Officers (£39m), Special Constables (£8m), the Street Crime Initiative (£25m), Reform Implementation (£8m), Non-Emergency Numbers (£3m), the National Intelligence Model (£2m), Counter-Terrorism (not given) and the Airwaves Communication Project (£58m).

24 See 'Going Local: Who Should Run Britain's Police', Barry Loveday and Anna Reid, Policy Exchange 2003 for an extensive discussion. Very often in US cities, the mayor is the effective purchaser. Around 44% of US cities have mayors and typically their powers extend to hiring and firing the police chief and setting the budget (although typically, this must be approved by a council).

25 Home Office (2001), *Policing a New Century: A Blueprint for Reform*.

• The Crime And Disorder Reduction Partnerships introduced in the Crime & Disorder Act stipulate that nationwide, police authorities and local councils are required to coordinate their activities with the production of crime prevention plans.

• The National Intelligence Model (NIM) launched in 2000 codifies an approach to policing that is already widespread but which may entail realigning existing resources and procedures for some forces, and should be adopted by all forces to commonly accepted 'minimum standards' by April 2004.

Policing: markets and management in practice

Any proponent of reinvention will, though, be under-whelmed by the rest of the record on the police. Choice mechanisms are absent, funding bears little relationship to performance or local priorities and corporate governance arrangements are so byzantine that it would be very hard to argue that they act as a driver for value for money, service improvement or indeed much else. The doctrine of 'operational independence' is perhaps the one redeeming characteristic of the system bringing with it as it appears to do, the reality that a local chief constable is free to manage.

A purchaser-provider structure was never brought into the police service during the Thatcher-Major public service reforms, despite its widespread use in the United States[24]. The 1994 Police and Magistrate's Courts Act consolidated the position of local police forces as local monopolies lightly touched by Police Authorities which are comprised of local councillors, Justices of the Peace and 'lay members' (no-one is directly elected of course). They are responsible for choosing Chief Constables (albeit from a Home Office shortlist), agreeing the Chief Constable's Police Plan and monitoring performance.

The government *has* begun moves in the right direction. A measure of deregulation now allows local authorities to act as purchasers of security services for particular forms of offence – such as environmental offences or anti-social behaviour. This was enabled by the police reform White Paper[25] which included powers for chief officers to accredit organisations, including community groups and private security staff, that are part of the "extended police family". These organisations would have access to police intelligence, co-ordination from the local beat manager and police command and control, but no powers of arrest. Thus, a chief officer could arrange local patrolling from a community group. The number of local wardens is now expanding very quickly and they are proving extremely popular.

Funding unfortunately remains wedded to inputs. Police funding is driven by a bureaucratic assessment of local need. Half of the money comes from the Principal Formula Police Grant (£4,288m in 2003/04), based on the resident and daytime population of the area, with adjustments for a dense or sparse population, deprivation and the amount of roads. The other half comes from a Standard Spending Assessment (another Whitehall-defined estimate based on a similar formula) but levied on local council tax payers who have little meaningful power of veto. Strangely, where there is a closer link between locally expressed preference and street level action – such as in local council's appointment of wardens - funding is provided by time-limited budgets such as Neighbourhood Renewal Funds.

The chief virtue of what is an otherwise highly regulated system is the doctrine of operational independence. The challenge however is that when priorities are set so clearly from Whitehall – in the form of Best Value targets – and when local corporate governance is so removed from direct pressure (few county council members of a police authority have been voted out on the grounds of a police force under-delivering), operational independence can be risky. Certainly, innovation in harnessing private (or not for profit) resources has been limited. Few secondary markets have emerged to support policing services such as facilities or asset management, or support functions. Deal flow is limited. Examples, such as the £120m PFI deal between Equion and the Metropolitan Police providing a 50 staff transfer to Equion, to do jobs like manning reception, administering custody suites, and managing property store rooms, are rare.

Local Government: markets and management in theory
Local councils employ 2.2 million people (twice as many as the NHS), spend £69.5 billion a year, 25% of all public expenditure in England[26], and their satisfaction score stood at 47% in 2002[27], a number which is falling for services such as street lighting, street cleaning and recycling facilities.

Like primary care trusts and the constabulary, the local council is effectively a local service monopoly. It is, of course,

26 Of which 41% finances education, and 19% funds social services.

27 MORI's People's Panel.

28 Local Government White Paper, 'Strong Local Leadership – Quality Public Services'.

29 Currently there are 22 excellent councils.

30 in the 1999 Local Government Act.

31 By November 2003 around 250 PFI projects had been endorsed across England by the inter-departmental Project Review Team.

distinguished by the very fact that its corporate governors are elected. Unfortunately, this is not perhaps the motive force it might be as British local government suffers what is in Europe a unique gap between turnout at local and national elections. As a consequence, the government has sought to strengthen the accountability and political management system for local councils. The Modernising Local Government Act enabled local councils to introduce a range of more effective political management systems such as mayors and the leader plus cabinet model.

This has been underpinned by an updated doctrine of local operations which has two important attributes. First, it is now much easier for local electors to understand how well their local council is doing. Comprehensive Performance Assessment (CPA), introduced in December 2001[28], draws together evidence from a wide range of assessments such as reports from Ofsted, the Social Services Inspectorate and the Benefit Fraud Inspectorate. CPA adds an audit report and a corporate governance assessment. The result is a balanced scorecard and assignment of the council to one of five categories; excellent, good, fair, weak or poor[29]. Second, the new regime brings with it new flexibilities, managerial and financial. The system of credit approvals has been abolished and replaced with a local prudential regime. Individual authorities are now responsible for deciding how much they can afford to borrow.

The replacement of compulsory competitive tendering with the Best Value regime[30] has been another important change. While retaining the purchaser-provider split in key areas of council operation, the obligation to put services out to competitive tender has been replaced by the duty of Best Value. Councils must prove to the Audit Commission that reviews are rigorous. The Audit Commission conducts – and publishes – its own assessments. The virtue of the system is that there is at least some institutionalised momentum forcing councils to consider questions about how to harness the market – both in the field of asset management and support services. As a result, the Private Finance Initiative (PFI) is now quite widespread[31]. There are, however, remaining problems. Local authorities are still very poor at controlling process costs, at benchmarking against comparable private sector organisations and the asset accounting rules do foster a relentless focus on asset management.

Local Government: markets and management in practice
In practice, this regime still has two significant flaws. First, the funding provides little reinforcement of the local accountability device. Councils are funded through three sources: 52% comes from central government, 22% comes from non-domestic rates, also set centrally, and only 26% comes from the council tax. Only a quarter of the available money actually comes from the affected populace. There is a related problem here of political monopoly. If the local council does indeed keep up the pressure on the management of specific services, this is invisible to most voters. Local electors unfortunately must rely on a more remote process. The Audit Commission, for example, must write a report about a failure that is often all too obvious to the electorate. Local voters must then hope that the council takes some corrective action. This is a bureaucratic and slow resolution procedure. Individual wards cannot, for example, simply decide to 'fire' a council's local environmental services providers if it is not any good and use their share of the money to hire their own.

The government's response has been to create a set of new organisations designed to foster partnerships between the many agencies at work in local government, notably Local Strategic Partnerships (LSPs). Created to bring together public, private and voluntary sector service providers with the community and business sectors, LSPs aim to co-ordinate national and local initiatives. Authorities that have established an LSP and agreed a neighbourhood renewal strategy are then eligible to receive grants from the Neighbourhood Renewal Fund. Alongside this, a plethora of initiatives has been established to nurture community renewal. The Community Empowerment Fund, Community Chest and Community Champions Fund are all now operating and the government has frequently expressed a desire for more use of area forums, public assemblies, citizen-user boards and advisory referenda. A statutory framework however has not yet been tabled.

The second persistent flaw concerns local regulation. Deregulation has been discussed but little yet delivered. One salutary exception is that local authorities now have some flexibility on supplying and charging for goods and services to others in the public, private and voluntary sectors. This measure was intended to replace reliance on the Local

Authorities (Goods and Services) Act 1970, which restricted local authorities' trading powers to dealings with other authorities and other public bodies. However, there is a great deal more that could be done. Councils which earn an 'excellent' score in the CPA have been promised a battery of new freedoms:

• fewer planning requirements

• financial freedoms

• more discretion over best value reviews

• a much lighter touch inspection regime

• the widest freedom to trade across their services

• a right to have existing ring-fenced grants replaced by targeted grants in any case where the council and government judge it to be desirable (except in respect of grants which have to be passed to schools)

• not being subject to the reserve powers to cap council tax increases

• more freedom to use income from fines (complete freedom for littering, parking) and a reduction in the proportion of ring-fencing of government support for capital investment (reform of the single capital pot).

Many of these are excellent ideas. It is a shame that no date for implementation has yet arrived.

Councils are funded through three sources: 52% comes from central government, 22% comes from non-domestic rates, also set centrally, and only 26% comes from the council tax. Only a quarter of the available money actually comes from the affected populace.

	Primary Health	LEAs	Police	Social services	Local Government	Acute Health	Schools
Choice	No choice of GP	No	No	Limited	No	Yes. GPs chose surgeons and trusts	Yes
Funding	Capitated	Capitated	Mixed. Rate Support grant (RSG) local taxes	Capitated to purchasing authority. But follows patient	Mixed. RSG + local taxes	Will follow demand. National tariffs	Follows pupil
Funding link to performance	No	No	No	No	To an extent	Yes	Yes
Competition	No	No	No	Yes. Demand placed with competitive supply chain	Limited. Best Value forces market testing	Yes. Including private sector and abroad	Limited by capacity
Purchaser-provider split	No	Mixed	No	Yes	Yes – in places	Yes	No
Separation of asset and operations	Yes. Assets often GP owned	No	No.	Yes. Private supply	Some – with PFI	Some – with PFI	No
Separation of front and back office	To an extent	No	Very limited	Yes. Private supply	Some – with PPPs	Some outsourcing	Limited
Accountability	League tables and CHI	League tables and Ofsted	League tables	Star ratings and SSI	CPA and Audit Commission	League tables and CHI	League tables and Ofsted
National targets	Yes. National Service	Yes	Yes	Yes	Yes	Yes. NSFs	Yes
Corporate governance	Frameworks (NSF) Board appointed	Indirect election	Mixed boards	Elected	Election	Board required to break even	Mixed board
Leadership	NHS Leadership programme	Organisation for local government	National Police Leadership Centre	NHS. DWP Gold	National Graduate Programme	NHS	The National College for School Leadership

Conclusion

We do not yet have public services that would be recognisable to a proponent of the principles of *Reinventing Government*. For all the undoubted moves in that direction, by successive governments, the rate of change has been slow. Perhaps this is to be expected. Public services are part of the democratic state and consent needs to be won over a long period if the reforms then embarked upon are to endure. It is to be hoped that reinventing government can itself be invented over again.

Chapter Two
Greater And Greater
Expectations

Gideon Skinner, James Crabtree, McKinsey Health Team

Executive summary

Gideon Skinner

Public services have been the main public concern for a decade but our expectations of services are changing – satisfaction has been stable since 1997 – GPs and schools do well, street services badly - it is very difficult to prove that expectations are, in fact, rising – there are signs that people expect education and policing to improve and MORI analysis of the NHS does suggest that the middle classes are becoming less satisfied at a time when outcomes are improving – this may be because they are comparing the service to the private sector – people want privacy, good respect, dignity and cleanliness from the NHS – they want be taken seriously, treated fairly and responded to quickly by the police.

Choice resonates strongly with people who see it as power being given back to them and gives providers an incentive to improve – but people also worry about equal provision and are concerned about the sorting effects that may occur in choice systems – in health care people wanted some help in making their choices, usually from a GP – people also want to be able to contact public services by various means and at their own convenience – for example, people favour police "shops" in town centres or information points in supermarkets - they are also aware they need good information to be able to act and

they often do not feel they receive it - people's expectations of
the state are different from their requirements from the market –
the idea of public value is a broad concept that attempts to
capture all the various requirements we have of public services.

James Crabtree

Will the digital generation expect more from public services
than can reasonably be delivered? – the public services now
understand the need to know their customers but can they
ever meet their demands? – citizens are far better informed than
they used to be – and the experience of service improvements
in the private sector has transformed their expectations –
perhaps disappointment is endemic for customers as our
expectations of all sectors rise in excess of their capacity.

The solution must be to implicate citizens in the provision
of public services – this can help to regulate demands and
expectations and might help to avoid policy errors such as the
rush to put government services online – no account was taken
of the demand for services or the type of service required by
those who were interested in e-government – the upshot was
that many pointless services were put online to a minimum
standard – the e-government citizens panel in Islington is
one way in which this can be avoided and one way in which
government can start to understand its customers better –
Milton Keynes council held a referendum on its budget which
involved citizens and created legitimacy and reasonable hopes
for the decision reached – universal electronic voting will
vastly lower the costs of such exercises.

McKinsey Health Team

Change to health services between now and 2020 will be
driven by more affluent, better educated, better informed,
busier patients, with higher expectations that their convenience
should be met - they will also compare the NHS more to
private providers – they will thus expect better and faster medical
treatment with quicker rates of recovery and more choices –
people will be prepared to pay more for health products.

There will be five consequences: people will expect greatly
reduced waiting times; a service that is up to date with the latest
diagnostic techniques and treatments; better food and sleeping

conditions than are currently available; a system whose constituent parts are adequately linked and a service far more tailored to their individual requirements.

Are expectations rising?
Gideon Skinner

Public services have been the public's main concern for a decade. The NHS in particular is now almost as totemic as inflation in the 1970s and unemployment in the 1980s[1]. Of course, public services do not exist in vacuum, and the society they serve has also changed over the last twenty years. We should expect that our needs and expectations of public services – and what we want them to do to improve – are also changing. While this is the case in some areas, the picture is more complex than might first appear. Here we look at these changes and the impact they may have, but also suggest that public services still have a unique relationship with the public.

Satisfaction with public services has been broadly stable since 1997. GPs and schools remain relatively highly rated by users while road and pavement maintenance still get the lowest scores. Local bus services, museums and the Passport Agency have all seen significant rises in satisfaction. Some street services have declined[2].

Whether expectations really are rising inexorably is tricky to prove – for example, it seems strange to argue that people expect the police to solve crime, health services to cure illness, or schools to educate our children now, but not twenty years ago. Moreover, satisfaction with different services varies – for some it stays stable, others fall and rise – which does not fit in with an idea of permanently rising expectations that become progressively harder to meet.

On the other hand, people do expect the quality of education and policing to improve over the next few years. MORI analysis of views of the NHS[3] suggests that the middle classes are becoming less satisfied with the quality of service the NHS provides. How is this the case when outcomes (measured in terms of life expectancy) are improving? This is especially curious when we consider that the middle-classes actually get

1 MORI Political Monitor.

2 *Monitoring Satisfaction: Trends from 1998 – 2002*, MORI People's Panel research for the Office of Public Services Reform.

3 MORI long term trends report.

4 *Is the NHS equitable*, Dixon, Le Grand, Henderson, Murray and Poteliakhoff. LSE Health And Social Care Discussion Paper 11 (2003)

5 MORI SRI analysis of survey data for the Commission for Health Improvement, 2004.

6 *Contacting The Police*, MORI SRI research for the Office of Public Services Reform, February 2003.

7 PIU Discussion Paper *Satisfaction with Public Services*, Donovan, Brown and Bellulo November 2001.

better treatment from the NHS than poorer groups[4]. It may be that satisfaction is falling because of rising expectations among the middle classes, perhaps partly because of greater exposure to private health care. So, even if expectations of outcomes have not changed *per se*, there is some evidence that the nature of people's demands have changed, particularly around service delivery and especially where people can make comparisons.

What is it that people specifically want from customer service? In the NHS they want privacy, they want to be treated with dignity and respect, they want good explanations and cleanliness[5]. From the police, people want to feel that they have been treated fairly, to be taken seriously and to receive a speedy response. It is also important that people find the police easy to get hold of and that they are kept informed of the progress of their case[6.]

We will focus here on two areas of change: (i) increasing choice and (ii) easier access to public services. Throughout this discussion, it is crucial to bear in mind that different groups in society move at different speeds. For example, some will embrace the use of new technology, and others will be much more comfortable with face-to-face contact. Some people are happy taking decisions for themselves, while others will look for more guidance from professionals. This diversity makes it even harder for public services to meet all these different demands.

Choice

As a concept, choice resonates very strongly with users of public services (particularly choice for individuals, as opposed to choice for providers such as government having a choice of contractor). Qualitative research suggests that it is associated with giving power back to the individual, giving services an incentive to improve the standards of service they provide, and more simply allowing users to choose the "best fit" for them personally. People do not feel that there is much real choice in public services at the moment, and do find it an attractive idea (in an extreme case, by refusing to pay council tax for services that do not reach certain standards). There is also some evidence from pilots in public transport from Australia and education in Milwaukee that increasing choice can lead to higher satisfaction with services[7]. But these demands, even for a concept as attractive as choice, need to be properly understood.

First of all, choice is still seen as a second-order priority by the public. The first step is to raise basic standards across the board; there is still support for the idea of equal provision, and concern about "postcode lotteries". People also recognise that there may be problems with greater choice. For example, they feel that it may lead to some schools/GPs being oversubscribed, while other areas risk becoming ghettos. To be able to make an effective choice also requires that everyone has access to similar information. Furthermore, in our health research we have found that only a minority of people want to make a choice of hospital unaided[8]. Most – over three in five – want some advice and information to help them make that choice. That advice needs to come from a trusted source (a GP or similar figure), underlining the relatively high levels of trust that people still place in some public service professionals. Again there are different attitudes to choice across the population, with older people much more likely to say that the decision should be left to the professional.

Access

An area where it is easier to see the impact of more choice is the demand for wider methods of access. Even in an area as sensitive as voting, and even among people who say that they personally want to continue voting in a polling station, there is an expectation that different methods will be open to those who want to use them[9]. The key issue here again is choice – people expect to be given a range of methods for getting in touch with public services, not just face-to-face but also by telephone, letter, and increasingly email and internet.

Similarly, there is strong support for the idea of one-stop shops and call-centres, another example of our expectations being raised by experience outside the public sector[10]. People also want to be able to access public services at weekends and after work (though not necessarily 24x7)[11], half expect a phone call to be answered within 10 rings, and half of internet users expect an email to be answered within 24 hours[12]. The public is open to communicating with the police, for example, by various means. For example, people are favourable towards the idea of police "shops" in town centres or contact points in supermarkets. These facilities re-assure the public and provide an ideal point of contact for the exchange of information.

8 MORI, 'Patient Choice in Birmingham, Solihull, and the Black Country', Research conducted for the Birmingham and the Black Country Strategic Health Authority, November 2003.

9 MORI, 'Public Opinion and the 2003 Electoral Pilot Schemes, Research Study conducted for the Electoral Commission', May 2003.

10 People's Panel, the Cabinet Office, 1st wave research, October 1998.

11 People's panel wave 4 October – December 1999.

12 People's panel wave 3 April 1999.

13 People's Panel, the Cabinet Office, 1st wave research, October 1998.

14 *Trust in Public Institutions*, MORI research for the Audit Commission 2002.

15 See the chapter by Greg Wilkinson in this volume. See also *Creating public value*, Kelly and Muers, Strategy Unit Discussion Paper, 2003.

Information

A pre-condition of both choice and access is that public services provide reliable and plentiful information. Public services are perceived to be poor at this. People are twice as likely to say that the private sector is better at providing information and this tendency is especially marked amongst the middle class[13]. People recognise that they need better information to make a valid choice. As one focus group participant put it, "We are intelligent people, we can make up our own minds after hearing the facts. Provided we do hear the facts".

Citizen-consumers

Public services, however, cannot meet these demands for more choice and better access simply by treating users as "private sector" consumers. This could worsen the feelings of disconnection between individuals and institutions discovered elsewhere[14]. People *do* have different expectations of public services then of private companies, even though many elements of the traditional view of a public service ethos are also shared – and often bettered – by customer service in the private sector. People judge public services twice, as users and as citizens. This is not to advocate a return to a provider-centric outlook, but to suggest that a broader conception of "the consumer" is necessary to rebuild some of this lost trust.

The concept of public value provides a framework for developing the relationship between public services and citizens[15]. It argues that public services need to take a holistic view of how they add value, by looking at service quality, final outcomes, and the impact on trust and confidence in public institutions. It suggests that public services need to be flexible, in their objectives (service quality, outcomes, trust etc), in the way they provide services, and in the way they take account and respond to people's needs (as users, as taxpayers, and as citizens with wider social concerns). It may be that this is the direction public services need to move in, if they are going to meet customer expectations while retaining the special status (and the benefits that this provides) that they have in the public mind. The concept of public value is a useful one to remind managers and policy makers the importance of the "public" in public services, the next step is to come up with some practical ways in which this can improve the service that is provided.

Googling Public Services
James Crabtree

What will the generation who grew up digital want from public services? Will they expect too much? The British online retailer Ocado suggested as much in 2003 advertising campaign featuring a sulking child under the headline "when did you stop being so demanding?" The message was clear: consumers were encouraged to demand high standards; Ocado would satisfy them. The deeper implication was disturbing. In the future organisations should expect adults to behave like children, to demand whatever they felt like without any consideration for resources or possibilities.

This is a worst-case scenario for public service managers. Osborne and Gaebler recognised the danger in Chapter Six of *Reinventing Government*, noting that "few people in Government ever use the word customer"[1]. They suggested that public sector organisations responded not to those they were meant to serve but to those from whom they received funding, trading off the interests of citizens in exchange for budgets and finance. A decade on and their suggestions have certainly taken hold. Typing "Citizen Focused" into Google now returns more than eight hundred thousand webpages of government strategies designed to re-orientate services around customers. Today the public sector knows it needs to understand its customers. The fear is it may never be able to satisfy them.

There are two problems here. First, there is good evidence that citizens are today better informed, more likely to complain, more likely to question the judgements of those in positions of authority. A survey from the PEW Internet Research Institute, for instance, found that 55% of those who use the internet to check for health information (22 million Americans) consulted the internet before visiting their doctors. 79% did the same after their visit[2]. The next generation of public service users – those from Generation Y, born between 1979 and 1994 – will consult Google first, their GP second.

Second, this coming generation's experience of the best services available in the private sector will reflect badly on those available from the state. In the time that it has taken

1 Osborne, T. and Gaebler D (1993) *Reinventing Government: How the Entrepreneurial Spirit is Transforming the Public Sector*, Penguin Books, New York.

2 The Pew Internet and American Life Project, Internet Health Resources, 2003 http://www.pewinternet.org/reports/toc.asp?Report=95.

3 Zuboff, S. and Maxmin, J. (2003) *The Support Economy, Why Corporations Are Failing Individuals and The Next Episode of Capitalism*, Penguin Books, London.

government to put most of its services onto the internet – most of which do not even allow full transaction – the private sector has thoroughly modernised what it means to order a book, send a parcel, or pay a bill.

But even here there are problems. Zuboff and Maxmin's *The Support Economy* suggests a total collapse in customer confidence, with even business attempts to satisfy customers unravelling. "At the start of the twenty first century" they argue "people have new dreams … expressed in a psychological awareness of one's own complex individuality…. As a result of these new dreams a chasm has opened up between people and the organisations in which they depend"[3]. Customers expecting a high quality of service find their expectations exceed that which organisations are capable of offering. Attempts to cope often only push cost, either financial or time, back onto the users themselves. The bank used to transfer money for you, now you do it yourself online; the bank manager used to call you back, now you have to wait on hold. No amount of business process re-engineering, total quality management or mass customisation, it seems, can stem customer disappointment.

Implicating Citizens

Yet even if the outlook for the private sector is this challenging we do not have to believe that the public sector's modernisation task is futile. What is needed, instead, are new mechanisms of *involving and implicating* citizens in the making of public decisions. Public service professionals must find better ways to involve citizens by keeping in touch with, and responding to, their concerns. Subsequently managers need to find ways of ratifying decisions by implicating customers and citizens in decisions in order to manage expectations of service levels. These can form the basis for a continuation of reinvented government in the face of raised citizen expectations. Osborne and Gaebler proposed techniques of customer engagement such as the provision of funding to individuals to allow them to chose service providers. Yet today these techniques are not sufficiently widely used.

Take the example of the current UK Government's strategy for the delivery of electronic services. This contained two significant strategic errors, both rooted in inadequate understanding of customer preferences. First, it set a target to put 100% of government services online without first prioritising the type of access channels citizens wanted to use. MORI evidence subsequently proved that very few citizens actually wanted to use the web as their primary channel of interaction with government. Most people prefer the telephone[4]. Thus while some service providers – for instance Liverpool Council's excellent *Liverpool Direct* – invested in sophisticated consumer-friendly call centres, many others put up websites which citizens didn't want. Second, the strategy didn't identify the services that people wanted to use on the web. So instead of focusing on services that suited the web, or suited those citizens who like to use the web, the exercise turned into a rush to tick boxes in project reviews by putting everything online to the minimum possible standard. It took the government a couple of years to realise that they were not delivering what their customers wanted.

4 Quoted in Crabtree, J. and Curthoys, N. (2003) *SmartGov: Renewing Electronic Government for Improved Service Delivery*, iSociety, The Work Foundation.

Public service organisations must learn from such mistakes. What *The Support Economy* calls the process of "discovering the end customer over and over again" should become the watch-word for managers. Islington Council's decision to launch an e-government citizens panel, in which over 100 local citizens will be involved in the design and development of local e-Government services, suggests a model of what can be done. Equally, public service managers should be encouraged to use more adventurous research techniques to understand how they can make government convenient and relevant to citizens. Just as anthropology has become a popular mechanism for business to understand precisely how their customers live their lives day-to-day, so the public sector should attempt to go beyond the consultation and surveying mechanisms outlined in *Reinventing Government* ten years ago.

Popular choice

This kind of process would also implicate citizens in public service decisions. Demanding citizens must be engaged in new, and potentially radical, processes of consultation that both manage expectations and create legitimacy for reform. This is exactly what Milton Keynes Council did in February 1999 in undertaking a referendum on its 1999/2000 budget. The

5 For a discussion of the referendum see http://www.laria.gov.uk/content/features/60/feat6.htm.

6 Kamarck, C. (2002) *Applying 21st Century Government to the Challenge of Homeland Security*, paper published by The PricewaterhouseCoopers Endowments for The Business of Government series.

Council laid out three options for tax rises and associated spending decisions[5]. In so doing they were asking a grown-up question on a specific issue: if you let us raise these taxes, we will spend it on these things and deliver these services. Citizens responded: nearly half the electorate voted, and decided on a modest tax rise in exchange for improved service. The council created a new contract with their electorate on an issue of public management, educated citizens about their choices, and laid out the terms on which the decision was to be made.

Universal electronic voting, likely within the next two decades, will vastly lower the cost of such consultative referenda. Harvard academic Elaine Kamarck, previously head of the Clinton Administration's National Performance Review programme, notes that "without information technology the competing demands of the public's 'Do This' but 'Don't let the government do that' would be impossible to meet"[6]. Over the next 20 years this insight will be as true in consultation as it will be in the delivery of service. Instead of pandering to the fears of direct democracy, public service decision makers should welcome the opportunity to ratify difficult decisions, engage with larger groups of citizens, and create new "citizen contracts" for modernisation. In so doing the public sector can counter the Ocado effect. Involving and implicating citizens, or treating users of public services as adults rather than expecting them to act like children, is the only firm starting point to continue reinventing government.

Healthcare 2020
McKinsey Health Team

The factors driving change to health services between now and 2020 can be grouped under three main headings:

(i) socio-economic trends

(ii) medical trends

(iii) increasing patient activism.

Socio-economic trends

Patients will be more affluent and the current middle-aged group will by then have far higher accumulated wealth and higher expectations of services. Alongside this, inequality or diversity in incomes will continue. People will become better educated, though with increasingly less time, resulting in them wanting more convenience tailored to their individual needs. As a result of all these changes, plus the influence of other cultures, people will be even less deferential. The elderly in particular will be less easily satisfied than their predecessors, but they will not be unique: already today consumers are more willing to complain. As people become more exposed to the standards of modern service industries, they are more able to compare the NHS against these standards.

Medical trends
We live in an environment of greater medical success, where the public expects better and faster rates of recovery for more medical conditions, with a greater choice of treatments. Patients will become better informed: there will be more channels through which content can be delivered and more active propagation of the information that is available. This propagation will come about not just through the growth in information sources, but also from the medical profession itself, and the media, which is constantly raising awareness of other systems particularly in Europe.

Increasing patient activism
Greater personal accountability will continue, as individuals take an active interest in their health and are willing to pay for health-related services and products, but in 2020 they will still not be one-sized. One person's attitude towards health will still differ from another's and people will continue to use health-related services very differently.

Five greater expectations
If these beliefs about future behaviour are accurate, they tend to the following five conclusions for the service:

1. Waiting within reason
Patients will expect a timely service with greatly reduced wait-

ing times. On all measures of expectation (from the first GP appointment to being seen by a specialist and for investigations to be performed, and waiting and admission times in A & E) the UK lags badly behind Germany and France. In 2020, patients will be willing to wait within reason, but reasonableness will mean days or weeks rather than months. This is a fundamental shift from current levels of performance or any current targets on waiting times.

2. An up-to-date service

On a number of measures the UK compares poorly with those perceived to be the best (uptake of new treatments, application of new approaches, use of the latest technology for diagnostics and communication). Where, for example, the National Institute for Clinical Excellence (NICE) has provided guidance on whether treatment regimes are effective enough to justify adoption, early evidence suggests that the treatment uptake rate may fall short of international comparators. In 2020 patients will expect the best available treatment with the minimum variability of success. Alongside this, they will expect more emphasis on lifestyle, prevention and screening from the health service. This includes demanding the latest diagnostic test rather than a 'wait and see' policy; minimum testing undertaken by the NHS as a routine part of every examination; and sufficient time spent with health professionals whose accreditation must increasingly be publicly available.

3. 3 star hotel service

Should in-patient treatment be required, patients will expect healthy food and a healthy environment. This may not appear a huge challenge, but the NHS currently spends only two-thirds of the amount those individuals would spend on themselves on food at home. Meanwhile, cleanliness – or the lack of it – is a regular feature of media reporting and is apparently driven by chronic under-investment in buildings maintenance. Patients will also expect to stay with fewer people in the same room; again, the UK compares badly with the best.

4. A seamless, efficient service

There must be proper links between primary care and hospitals;

efficient communication between departments once in hospital; and effective links between the health service and other services on discharge from in-patient treatment. These connections do not operate as efficiently as they might; based on technological advance, the patient in 2020 will expect 'one system looking after my needs' with electronic access across disciplines to patient information and records.

5. A personalised service
While the UK government's commitment to a patient-centred service is not unique, delivering the implications of that may be. Here, expectations are based on more choice of physician and hospital, wider access rights and times, and a wider range of available treatments. This will include some services currently outside statutory NHS limits such as homeopathic regimes.

Chapter Three
Why The Left Should
Choose Choice

Niall Maclean, Ann Rossiter, Jonathan Williams

Executive Summary
Public services are not currently providing equal access or outcomes – extending user choice could empower everyone and ensure providers make better use of resources – the political left will object that this is not true, that choice mechanisms will widen inequality – this criticism is wrong – carefully designed choice systems can help equality – there are three common objections to choice systems: first, polarisation – good services get better, bad services get worse and the poor end up with the poor services – second, capability: the well-off and the articulate are able to exercise choices while the poor and the ill-informed are not – third, selection: providers will end up choosing and the outcome will be segregation.

These three objections can all be met. First, levelling-up: there is evidence from policy experiments in the USA and Sweden that well-designed school choice mechanisms can increase standards across all groups – funding and enrolment are competitive in both cases and selection of pupils is regulated – in both cases the surrounding public schools have responded by raising standards – in Michigan and Arizona in the USA parents were given a voucher which they could take to a charter school – when 6% did so, beneficial competitive effects were seen both to absolute standards and to productivity – the same happened when Sweden introduced competition into its school system, with no adverse effect on the poor.

Second, building capability: the existing system, characterised by voice mechanisms and by limited choice, significantly favours the middle class – in a system of choice for all some may not want to choose and this choice should be respected – they may delegate their choice to an expert agent like a GP – people should be given the information and support required to be able to exercise choice – a network of qualified agents would help to minimise bad choices and to equalise the capacity to make good choices – the NHS choice pilots are an example of supported choice in practice where take-up of choice, mediated by a Patient Care Advisor, has been very popular across all social classes – this contrasts with the experience in France where less care was taken to design policy to preserve equity.

Third, priority for the worse-off: the temptation for providers to select the best users can be offset by regulation to deny them the right to choose or by limiting choice only to the worse-off citizens – priority for the worse-off can also be ensured by allowing more funding to attach to some classes of user – the Milwaukee voucher system introduced more competition for schools with a high proportion of students eligible for free school meals and the schools facing competition subsequently performed significantly better than those that did not – vouchers can be weighted in favour of the least well-off as indeed has happened in Dutch schools.

Introduction

Public services as they stand are not making as much of resources as they might do; they are allowing inequality to flow through them; and in some cases they are actually amplifying it[1]. It goes without saying that neither choice nor its absence is the remedy for all of these failings. However, increasing user choice in public services offers the twin promise of extending empowerment to everyone and ensuring that *all* providers make better use of resources.

The overwhelming objection from the left is that this is simply not true: even if choice might work for some areas, benefits will ultimately fall to the wrong people and choice will be at the expense of the individuals who need public services most. We want to take on this criticism. We do not just seek to argue that

1 See for example, *Is the NHS Equitable?: A review of the Evidence*, LSE Health and Social Care Discussion Paper Number 11, (London: The London School of Economics and Political Science, London), November 2003.

2 There are a number of different types of choice in operation in public services across the world, including the operation of collective choice by associations or groups of users, and the operation of choice of services from a single, usually monopoly provider. For the purposes of this essay, choice mechanisms should be taken to be those that offer individuals a choice of provider.

the use of choice mechanisms could result in improvements in the quality of public sector delivery. There is certainly some evidence to suggest they *could* achieve this, and the literature on this is large and growing. Our aim is more ambitious – we will argue that choice mechanisms are capable of making the *specific* sorts of improvements in our public services that reflect the core values of the left - equality, fairness and co-operation and support of public goods[2].

In this essay we argue that choice mechanisms provide the materials for an effective assault on inequality in public services. We will do this by confronting the three most thoughtful objections that are frequently levelled at choice mechanisms. We address each of these in turn, arguing that well-designed choice mechanisms would go a long way to making public services fairer and more equal than they are under the current situation of limited choice. We put the emphasis on *carefully designed* and we will go to some lengths to unpack exactly what we mean by this. It should come as no surprise to any of us that badly designed choice systems are capable of offending our values. Just as capable, in fact, as the status quo.

Objection One: Polarisation

Perhaps the most frequently voiced objection regarding choice mechanisms is that they result in well-performing public services getting better and badly-performing services getting worse. If funding follows the choices made by users, and if users choose well-performing over poorly-performing providers, then high-ranking schools and hospitals will systematically get more funding than those lower down the achievement scale. Limits to capacity mean that those individuals lucky enough to be able to choose the good schools and hospitals will get far better services than those stuck with poorly-performing ones. The gap in the relevant kind of outcomes (a decent education, good health) would widen. This is straight-forwardly an affront to the value of equality.

Objection Two: Capability

Almost as frequently voiced is the following objection: choice mechanisms by their very nature favour those who are best placed and best equipped to make good choices. These are usually middle-class, well-educated people, who have the confidence, expectations, contacts, savvy and of course the resources - transport, ability to take time off work, and so on – to make the most of the choices on offer. Moreover, not only would this kind of inequality between choosers widen the gap between better and worse-off service users, it would also exacerbate polarisation: the good schools will not only get more funding; they will also benefit from receiving the best choosers, who in all probability will be easier to teach as well as better-off.

Objection Three: Selection
This point leads naturally into the third most common objection – people are not only unequal in their capacity to make choices, they also impose different costs and benefits on public services. This gives rise to the wrong incentives: services are motivated to select the easiest to treat, or the easiest to teach. Service users, in turn, will be motivated to seek out providers that benefit from a population of better-off service users, because those services will have more to offer them. This is already true of course, in that the motive already exists. The problem is particularly serious for choice in education because pupils have a direct effect on one another's achievement. However the point is a general one - so long as worse-off service users impose greater costs on providers, both providers and other service users will be motivated to separate themselves from them. Again, if choice gives them greater means as well as motive to do so then it is likely to worsen inequality between service users.

> Osborne and Gaebler were evangelists for the virtues of competition, and by extension, choice. They argued that it led to the "survival of the helpful" and provided a vital motor force for improvement. They were also adamant that carefully-designed competition can improve equity and that services tailored to actual demands by citizens were inconceivable without it.

First Retort: Levelling-Up
The most basic objection to the extension of user choice was

3 Hoxby, C. (2003), 'School Choice and Competition: Evidence from the United States', *Swedish Economic Policy Review*, No. 2, pp. 9-65.

4 'School Choice Works' The case of Sweden', *Issues in Thought*, Schools Choice, Volume 1, Issue 1, Indianapolis, 2002.

that better services would get better and worse services would get worse, leading to inequality on the relevant outcomes as some would be stuck with poorly performing services. And this worry is felt particularly keenly for choice in schools, since it is believed that failing schools will be stripped of the pupils most likely to benefit their peers. However there is significant evidence – indeed it comes from experiments with school choice – that well-designed choice mechanisms create a 'levelling-up effect'; that is, the quality of service provision goes up *across the board*. Of course this outcome depends crucially on their design: flexibility in the supply of school places, the amount of money that follows pupils to and from schools, the relationship between that funding and the students or their schools' characteristics, whether or not schools can exercise selection, how parents and pupils are assisted in making choices[3]. Our argument is not that fairness and efficiency are the general outcomes of choice *per se* but that choice mechanisms can be designed to have consistent, predictable and desirable impacts in the places that most need it.

This is now being demonstrated in countries such as the USA and Sweden[4]. Although they have not in fact made efforts to weight every feature towards worse-off students, they have taken basic precautions to ensure equity and standards. Most importantly, in the USA and in Sweden funding and enrolment are on relatively competitive terms, and selection of pupils is both regulated against, but also minimised through flexibility on the supply side, which reduces the need for selection procedures for allocating scarce places. In each case *public* schools have responded to new competition by raising standards for their pupils. We begin with school choice reforms in Michigan and Arizona and then look at school choice at the national level in Sweden.

Both Michigan and Arizona enacted charter school reforms in 1994. Essentially, this means that they introduced a regulated voucher system into public education: so long as they met relevant standards, and agreed not to charge parents fees or to refuse entry to children with poorer prospects, charter schools would be eligible to receive state funding. If parents then decided to transfer students from their regular public school to a charter school, a significant share of the state's per pupil funding would

follow their choice – leaving the regular public school and
ending up with the charter school. And because both states
were (relatively) generous, both about funding and about
regulation, the reforms did generate effective competition in
some districts. The public schools in Michigan and Arizona
were used to natural variation in their student enrolment,
usually of about six percent per year, so it's unsurprising
that they didn't respond to competition until charter school
enrolment in their district hit the six percent level. When it
did, public schools responded by raising their achievement.

The Arizona public schools that faced competition from
charter schools raised their scores in 4th grade maths and reading
by 1.4 national percentile points per year. Public schools facing
competition in Michigan improved in the same exams, by
2.5 national percentile points per year[5]. Moreover, for both
Michigan and Arizona public schools that faced competition
from charter schools, the resulting improvement trends were
significantly better than in the period before competition was
introduced, and significantly better than the improvements
made in the same period by public schools that did not face
competition from charter schools. Finally, and most importantly, all of these improvements in *achievement* were mirrored by
improvements in *productivity*. They didn't improve simply
because they received extra funding. They improved by making
better use of funding they had.

Of course, these are relatively small and short-term effects,
from relatively low levels of competition. However they
certainly show that fears about polarisation may be misplaced.
The Swedish choice reforms in education, which were much
more extensive, add weight to this argument. By 1992 Sweden
had replaced a policy of almost total centralised provision in
education with a comprehensive system of *public* vouchers for
independent schools, with per pupil funding on roughly equal
terms. This produced a substantial response on the supply side:
before the reform in 1990 there were around 90 independent
schools. By 2003 the number of independent schools had
increased to 539, with 5.7% of pupils attending. As with
Michigan and Arizona, choice levered improvements in public
schools: competition from independent schools was consistently associated with public school improvements on achievement

5 The results focus on
4th grade maths and
reading because it was only
elementary schools that
lost a significant number of
students to charter schools,
and because the 4th grade
exam is the only national,
student-ranking exam at the
elementary level. In both
states elementary school
children are five times more
likely than secondary level
children to enrol in charter
schools. This is because the
per-pupil funding terms given
them by the state are on
the whole not sufficiently
generous to allow secondary
level charter schools to cover
their costs, particularly to
reach effective scale.

in mathematics. The likelihood of a student leaving school with no failing grades also fell.

Crucially, there was no adverse effect on low-achievers from public schools. Moreoever, improvements were not confined to the public schools. Competition has a significant and positive effect on achievement for *all* students - a ten percent increase in private school enrolment raised students mathematics scores by five percentiles in the national score distribution. And once again there was no significant difference in the impact of school competition on lower and higher performing students.

It is clear from these examples that school choice *can* be used to level up quality across the board. There are, certainly, counter-examples. The experience of school choice reforms in Chile and New Zealand was far less welcome, from an egalitarian point of view. There are two conclusions we can draw from these varied experiments: first, the design of policy has a strong, positive effect on outcomes for the worse-off; second, there is much more that we could do if we are to reform public services not just with consideration for worse-off service users, but with *priority* for worse off service users.

Second Retort: Building Capability
A large part of the critique of choice in public services is that it systematically favours those who are best equipped to make good choices. These people usually impose fewer costs on services and are better-off more generally. So as well as being unfair this also offends against equality (as the gap between middle classes and those lower on the socio-economic scale would widen).

However, it cannot be over-emphasised that public services where choice is not explicitly offered to all do anyway amplify inequalities between services users. Indeed, as Julian Le Grand has pointed out, critics of choice often make this point themselves: assuming they are giving examples of differential success through choice, whereas they are in fact giving examples of differential success through *voice*. The articulate middle class have always dominated voice mechanisms. Neither can it be emphasised enough that systems in which choice is restricted do not prevent services from amplifying inequality. This is because, in a system where choice is not explicitly valued and encouraged, *only* those who are capable of making clandestine choices will profit. Those who have the contacts, the knowledge, the language, the money, the confidence will be at a greater advantage. In short, the existing system of clandestine choice is set up to favour the middle class.

Now imagine a system of transparent choice, where all users are encouraged and equipped to choose. Again, this is where the importance of design comes in. It is obviously the case that some individuals simply don't want to choose, or are anxious about choosing, or feel ill-equipped to choose, or indeed might make bad choices. We take these concerns on board: a well designed choice system will recognise these facts and will actively help these individuals, rather than leaving them to navigate their way around the system. Those individuals who simply do not want to choose should have their choice – for choosing not to choose is a choice – respected. These individuals should feel free to delegate their choice to an intermediate agent, a GP for example. Those individuals who are anxious about choosing, or feel ill-equipped to choose, should be given the information and support required for them to feel (and, indeed to *be*) more capable of exercising choice. This might mean choosing in consultation with a qualified agent.

The provision of qualified navigators would also help minimise the effects of bad choices. However we should not shy away too much from the fact that some individuals will always make bad choices. They already do under the existing system – it is every citizen's right not to seek medical treatment or to ignore the advice of a doctor. We allow bad choices because we take seriously the value of individual freedom. The crucial point, however, is not the emphasis on individual freedom (which has, after all, been used to justify a great number of different views); the concern of the left is *effective* freedom. This is not the sort of freedom cherished by the right, where we simply create a space around the individual. This is a richer, more substantive notion, which acknowledges the need to foster the capacity to act freely. A well-designed choice system, which provides expert assistance to those who require it, does a great deal of justice to this notion. In short, we will have made a significant step towards an important left-wing goal – equalising the capacity to make good choices.

Although they are still at a relatively early stage, the NHS

6 Porell, F., & Adams, K. E., (1995), 'Hospital Choice Modeling: A conceptual review and evaluation of their utility for analysis of policy impacts', *Medical Care Research and Review*, 52, (2), 158-195.

choice pilots are the best examples of supported choice in practice. There are a number of pilots: the three largest are London, Manchester and the national scheme for patients awaiting cardiac surgery. The schemes offer a choice of at least one alternative provider to patients unlikely to be treated within six months at the hospital to which they were originally referred. Patients are contacted at around the five month period by a dedicated Patient Care Advisor (PCA), who informs patients of their choices, organises accommodation and transport for patients and their companions, and co-ordinates follow-up care. The cardiac scheme PCAs are clinically trained. In contrast to international experience – where patients have on the whole appeared unwilling to choose a more distant provider – take-up in all three is high. 67% of patients in the London pilot, 75% of patients in the Manchester scheme and 50% of the patients in the cardiac scheme took up the choice offered them. Crucially, preliminary analysis of the London data by PCT shows no significant relationship between the deprivation index of the PCT and the take-up of choice[6].

A recent survey of the national cardiac scheme suggests that the quality of PCA was crucial, both for the quality of choice patients' experience, but also for whether or not patients took up the choice in the first place. More than two-thirds of patients treated elsewhere reported that they had definitely received enough information on the hospital, on travel arrangements for themselves, and travel arrangements for their companions. This compares to less than half for the patients that turned down the choice. Patients who took up the choice were also more likely to answer favourably about their PCA in general: 61% of patients who travelled to an alternative hospital rated their PCA as 'excellent', compared to 37.9% for patients who remained on the waiting lists. This pattern was also mirrored in responses to other questions – on information (as above), on how easy it was to involve family and friends, and on how easy it was to keep in touch about treatment. Finally, comments on follow-up care were generally very favourable, and again 'it appears as if the PCAs played a key role in minimising difficulties and guiding patients through the system'. We take these preliminary results to confirm the point that if choice schemes are designed to ensure equity – in this case

equity between choosers – they can *do so*. This is all the more
so given that, if necessary, this kind of support can be targeted
towards the people who need it most.

Of course, the corollary of all this is also true: where
choice schemes are not designed to ensure equity between
choosers, there is not much reason to expect them to. A study
of patient choice in France, where choice is not supported
in these ways, found that patients with lower socio-economic
status (measured in a variety of ways) were all less likely to
travel further for care. Moreover take-up in general has been
low, and this also is in part because patients have not been
adequately informed of the choices available to them,
or adequately supported in taking advantage of them.
By contrast, take-up of patient choice in the UK pilots has
been high, and the preliminary evidence is that it has not been
skewed by social status. The implication is that if we move
away from the existing system of clandestine choice to a system
of choice for all; that provides help to those who require it,
then we will have generated a substantial gain in terms of
fairness. The fact that more individuals will be capable of
making the good choices previously only enjoyed by the middle
class provides further grounds for thinking that, far from
exacerbating the gap in outcomes between the middle class
and the rest, a well designed choice system would do
something towards closing this gap.

Third Retort: Priority For The Worse-Off

A final and important objection to the extension of choice was
that it would give users and providers additional means for
distancing themselves from worse-off recipients. The motive is
of course already there: where service users impose different
costs on public services and on each other that services are not
adequately compensated for, then both providers and users
are likely to seek out and cultivate a population of less costly,
better off service users. The objection to choice is that it would
extend both the means and the motive for them to do so, thereby exacerbating inequality between service users. It is therefore
up to advocates of choice to show that the productivity benefits
of choice can be combined with an effective strategy for
dealing with this source of inequality.

7 See Hoxby, CM (2001), *Ideal Vouchers*, Paper prepared for delivery at the Inequality Summer Institute, Harvard University, June 13-14, 2001, for this point and many below.

Strategies of this kind fall into two main classes. First, there are policies based on *regulation*. Providers can be denied the option of choosing between recipients or, more radically, choice can be extended to the worse-off only, as with some school voucher policies in the USA. Second, there are policies based on funding. The idea here is that the amount of money following users varies with their characteristics, thereby reducing the impact that those characteristics have on their success within the system while maintaining the essential mechanisms of choice and contestability. The regulation strategy has the clear disadvantage that it restricts choice to a sub-set of service users. However this strategy has brought about dramatic benefits for worse-off students in schools in the USA, and these successes do demonstrate that competition can favour the worse off. So we begin by looking at the USA's targeted choice scheme before looking at the more general, funding-based strategy.

In 1990 Milwaukee enacted a voucher reform that allows public school students to transfer a proportion of state per-pupil funding to a private school should they choose to do so. However this offer was essentially notional until 1998, when the Supreme Court upheld the programme, thereby ensuring that students could attend religious schools (the majority of Milwaukee private schools operating at the voucher level are religious), and raising the enrolment ceiling from one to fifteen percent of pupils. At this point change was rapid: enrolment had sextupled by spring of that year, and competition became effective immediately. Public schools faced more or less competition depending on their proportion of students eligible for free school meals. For some schools this meant that nearly *all* of their students could in theory have been lost to a voucher school. Hoxby studied the effect of competition on the public schools, classing them according to the number of students in those schools eligible for a voucher. The schools 'most treated' by competition had over two thirds of students eligible for vouchers. The 'somewhat treated' schools had less than two thirds (but over 25%), and the 'untreated' schools – a control group of similar schools from an area of Wisconsin where the voucher was inapplicable - had no students eligible[7].

The results are striking. Although the schools that faced greater competition had far more students that were African

American, Hispanic or eligible for free school meals, they generated much larger improvements on their pre-competition scores in Mathematics, Science and Language than schools that faced less competition. While improvement gains remained flat or unimpressive in the control schools between 1997 and 2002, the most treated schools improved by eight national percentile points in Mathematics, fourteen in Science, and eight again in Language. The somewhat treated schools improved by six in Mathematics, eleven in Science, and six in Language. And importantly, these improvements in achievement are mirrored by achievements in productivity, confirming that these schools didn't simply raise their achievement by increasing their costs.

While we are not advocating here a system in which choice is restricted to a sub-set of service users, experiments such as these do make the important point that competition can favour worse-off service users. The crucial question is whether similar benefits can be obtained, not through restricting choice but through weighting the market in favour of the worse-off. If sensitivity in funding can turn the attention of providers towards worse-off citizens, then the benefits of universal choice would be combined meaningfully with the principle that we should give priority to the worse off in distributing benefits. The point is simply that weighted funding could provide an internal solution to the problem of different costs imposed by different service users, and that this could still come with the benefits of choice.

There are lots of variations on this theme. Vouchers can vary according to the user, the user's neighbourhood, the sending service, the receiving service and so on. They can also vary according to what we might call 'strength': some schemes will be intended to make a fundamental change in the motivations of service providers; others may be intended only as a way of compensating them for (naturally and willingly) attracting users that can only be helped at a greater cost.

Conclusion

There is no general outcome for choice in public services; the outcome depends upon the aims internalised in the policy. In public services we aim above all for fairness and efficiency.

We have argued that choice, extended in the right ways and with worse-off service users explicitly in mind, can bring about substantial benefits in both of these areas. It would be a shame if potentially powerful levers of policy were to be ruled out for ideological reasons that have no basis in the evidence. If we put our values first and then assess calmly which policies can help to realise them, it will be clear that carefully designed choice mechanisms can help to match the preferences of citizens to the services offered whilst increasing both efficiency and equity at the same time.

Chapter Four
Community-Owned
Government

Keith Ruddle, David Varney & Mary Harris

Executive Summary

Empowering communities is an important way of anticipating problems – it was an important theme in *Reinventing Government* and there have been many such schemes since 1997 – they fall into three categories: self-help, business as a catalyst and social enterprise – self-help schemes in Bromley-by-Bow, Newham and Cheltenham have been very responsive to local needs – it is vital to recognise that businesses will not be engaged unless the benefits are mutual – we need to consider whether such business involvement is a welcome bonus or should become systemic – social enterprise is an example of mutual benefit and it is flourishing but has several drawbacks, notably dealing with the lenders and suppliers of capital.

Arthritic institutional structures are often a barrier against innovation – regulation has the effect of stifling innovation and risk-tasking – we need individuals who are prepared to be rebels – the examples of good practice all relied on heterodox individuals who challenged the culture of dependency – this good practice rarely spreads, though – the incentives are wrong for it to do so and too many people retain a vested interest in the status quo – innovation has to be nurtured, leaders have to be found who are prepared to take risks and the political class needs to show long-term commitment.

In 1992, Osborne and Gaebler argued that strong community ownership of problems could lead to more effective government by focusing on the root cause rather than the symptoms. This chapter draws on the experience of some such initiatives over the last 10 years. Each one of them took place in spite of, rather than because of, the arthritic system. Each involved a range of non-state actors and each one requires the government, to use the term from *Reinventing Government*, to steer rather than row.

> Osborne and Gaebler recommended that involvement and citizenship need to replace dependency and passive clienthood. Government should entrust many functions to community organisations as they tend to be more committed and their representatives understand them better. They want to solve problems where governments blindly provide services. They deal with the causes rather than reacting expensively to the symptoms. Government should not compel communities into these roles but create structures and intermediary organisations to make them easier, like housing corporations owned by residents.

Anticipatory policy

The desire to empower communities to solve their own problems was a central argument of *Reinventing Government*. State-provided services can create a dependent culture and the remoteness of the state means that policy will rarely be relevant, flexible, creative or rapid. State-run policy is also less likely to understand the root causes of problems. Community self-help could, therefore, help to anticipate problems rather than merely respond and remedy.

Osborne and Gaebler provided many examples of this: neighbourhood policing owned by the community, public housing developments and fire prevention schemes. They showed that the United States (US) Environmental Protection Agency spent 99% of its budget managing pollution rather than preventing it. The US, they said, had been transformed from a nation of self-help organisations to one that relied on bureaucrats and professionals.

Anticipatory policy is temptingly attractive in the UK. It would be wonderful to nurture self-help and local ownership and thereby prevent problems before they surfaced and needed remedial action by the central state. It might, indeed, be thought that the launch, since 1997, of hundreds of community-based initiatives, action zones, partnerships and so on might be a sign of progress. Behind this activity, however, lies an important question: does the rest of the 'system' help or hinder such aims? Below, we consider three approaches, from which we take lessons and draw conclusions for policy.

1 Hazel Blears, Communities in Control, Fabian Society, 2003.

Self help

The Wanless Report estimated that increased understanding, knowledge, self-help and engagement in public health by the public over the next 20 years could save the NHS £30 billion every year by 2002 - nearly half its current budget. This theme was echoed by Hazel Blears in her recent paper *Communities in Control* [1].

> **Case Study One: Bromley-by-Bow Healthy Living Centre**
> This is a voluntary organisation that integrates services to over-come many of the traditional obstacles to good health care in deprived inner-city areas. The range of services include GPs, health visiting, community care, crèches, toy library, basic skills and vocational training, teenage parenting support, childcare, benefits advice, job clubs and language support.

There are important differences between schemes that are all, in one sense, self-help initiatives. In Bromley-by-Bow, local social entrepreneurs have been active in connecting with disaffected and disadvantaged groups and some of these groups' key members. The community activists have also taken a very active approach to matching funding, from public and private sources, to local needs.

> **Case Study Two: The Newham Food Access Partnership**
> This was established by local residents in 2001. There are now 16 food co-operatives, breakfast clubs in schools, a healthy food box scheme run alongside Sure Start for young families and a healthy cafe - all promoting health eating at affordable prices.

In Newham, in addition to the food co-operatives, truancy sweeps have helped tackle property crime, and car crime has been cut by 70%. Similarly in Blackburn, Youth Works, a skills and confidence building organisation for young people, has helped cut crime by 12%. In Cornwall, a joint venture between council, health authority and housing associations has organised insulation improvements cutting significantly respiratory problems of children.

Case Study Three: Health Action Centres, Cheltenham

There are areas of poverty, deprivation and long-term ill health in Cheltenham amidst the general affluence. Community-managed mental health support groups and eight health action centres based in the estates with surgeries to support all aspects of residents' lives have been supported by the co-operative movement. They have also developed a number of community enterprises creating jobs and self help.

Business as catalyst

The link between social outcomes and the return to the company is often tenuous. To suppose that business collaboration in policy objectives should be detached from their duty to their shareholders is naïve. Where businesses have successfully been involved in solving communal, policy questions, this connection has been explicit.

Case Study Four: Young Offenders in Reading Prison

This scheme was set up by the National Grid Transco (NGT) Foundation (originally established by BG in 1998 and then Lattice). It was originally aimed at 17-21 year olds in Reading Prison. There was a shortage of forklift truck drivers in the area and the company designed a training scheme for 100 people that led to a qualification and a placing in employment. Re-offending was significantly reduced. The pilot scheme at Reading was extended and the company have been actively aiming to replicate it in other places round the country. The company has brought expertise, networks and resources. Collaboration was required with the Prison, the Probation service, the Home Office, Skills Councils and local employers - some of whom were part of the NGT supply chain.

There is no doubt that there are some good examples in which the involvement of business has improved public services. This is particularly so when the business has a vested interest in the social outcomes sought. The expertise, business skills, leadership and vested enthusiasm do seem to be important. But there is an important question here: do we regard such involvement as a systemic part of the way change in public services can progress or is it just a bonus? If it is to become systemic there is a lot more we need to understand about how it works to produce and sustain change.

Case Study Five: Reading Creative Education (CRED) scheme
Each year 13000 children are excluded from school. NGT created a new 'school' on its own premises in Reading specifically for 50 excluded 14-16 year olds. The teenagers follow a work related curriculum, focusing on literacy, numeracy and GNVQ, with work experience organised by the local Education Business Partnership. Local companies, including NGT, their supply chain and others, provide placements and subsequent employment. Attendance went from 40% to 95%. This required collaboration between committed people from NGT, the LEA, schools, other companies and the Department for Education and Schools and considerable ingenuity on all their parts to secure both funding and legitimacy.

Social Enterprise
There is a set of initiatives which breaks down the distinction between the policy objective on the one hand and the business imperative on the other. They are usually described as social enterprises and now employ more people than the agricultural sector. In 2001 the Department of Trade and Industry established the Social Enterprise Unit and a £125m investment fund to help voluntary and community organisations. It is said that social enterprises might be ideally responsive local organisations in areas of policy such as child and elderly care, waste management, housing maintenance and local transport.

Case Study Six: Pack-IT, Cardiff

Pack-IT does contract packing fulfilment and despatch.
It is heavily staffed with local people with Down's syndrome
and others who are profoundly deaf or have behavioural
or learning difficulties. Turnover has reached £1.4m in nine
years. Everyone is on market rates, full time and profits
are ploughed back into the business. The project began in
1994 in Cardiff as a grant-aided social services project but
when Cardiff County Council withdrew its grant the new
managing director decided to 'kick the grant dependency'.
It is remarkable example of a local authority social services
project that became a trading company.

Social enterprise has its roots in the 19th century cooperative
movement. Profits are ploughed back into the business rather
than distributed to shareholders or directors. These models are
not without major drawbacks - not least in dealing with the
lenders and suppliers of capital, the regulators of enterprise,
and the procedures of bidding for public contracts when often
one-year contracts are the norm with no security of tenure.

The Arthritic System and The Rebels

What do these experiences tell us about the barriers to
progress? These initiatives, by their nature, take time, require
multiple resources to attack the root causes, and inevitably
come up against the existing models of public sector management and behaviour. Many of them have to get funding and
legitimacy from the authorities involved. You cannot set up a
new school for excluded children without fitting somehow in
with LEA budgets, school roll procedures, DfES, health safety
and social service rules and regulations. All such mechanisms
have been designed for a good purpose but they have the effect
of stifling innovation. Managers are also discouraged from taking risks. Their attitude has ranged from wholehearted support,
to guarded enthusiasm, to benevolent but uncommitted critique,
to suspicion, to downright hostility. All of them are also
bounded (or feel they are bounded) by the system in which
they work. This might seem a negative view, but those who
have been part of these initiatives often talk about 'arthritic

structures', a culture of risk avoidance, challenges of joining up budgets and objectives across agencies, and a real challenge to get the money to the bits of the new emerging world that seem to be working – often against the system.

Individual rebellion is an important part of progress. The initiatives in Reading, Bromley and Newham started with a sense of outrage that the system was failing and the culture of dependency that it encourages. Dependency is endemic – on grants, on public handouts, on an array of support services, rained down on local needs, often unconnected and with no incentive to solve the real underlying problem that created the dependency in the first place. In many examples the 'outrage' and urge to solve the problems came from those not part of the 'dependency provision': from businesses who could see the benefits to themselves and individual leaders who simply could not allow the problems to fester. All of these initiatives were started by individuals who challenged the orthodoxy. They found some energy and resource and pulled resources and allies to the cause. All of the examples required working hard at getting the confidence of the key groups involved (the ill, the excluded, the offenders, and the disaffected) and engaging them in helping themselves.

Good Practice Never Spreads
Many of the examples quoted have come to public light through local success, plaudits, awards and a plethora of senior civil servants and ministers visiting and anointing the trailblazers. The Audit Commission has itself joined the game by identifying best practices in local government in solving local problems. There is often nothing more rewarding for those involved, including businesses and voluntary bodies who have taken a lead, than the glow of official approval.

But the spread of good practice or rather the lack of it, is a source of major frustration. The experiments above show that it is possible to develop a business model that works, that gets at root causes and that lifts the dependency gloom. Why can these models not be replicated across the country? Why don't the established institutional mechanisms cope with take-up and replication? Why are the incentives still all wrong?

In other fields of public sector innovation – for example in health and education – there are major investments in practice and knowledge sharing processes. However, the replication of innovation remains frustratingly slow. The basic truth is that, as Michael Bichard has pointed out elsewhere in this book, too many levels in the system have a vested interest in the status quo.

Case Study Seven: The Regulations Governing School Capacity

The regulations governing school openings, closures and expansions are considered by the Schools Organisation Committee (SOC), an independent body appointed by the Local Education Authority (LEA) and responsible for the School Organisation Plan in the area. The requirements on the SOCs are stringent and refer much more widely than the single issue of school closure. They must publish any proposal for a new community, foundation or voluntary school or for a school to be enlarged by a certain amount. Proposals must also be published where it is planned to close a school; to transfer to a new site; to add or remove a sixth form; to add or remove special educational needs provision; to change from single to mixed sex or vice versa; to end selection at a grammar school; to change school category.

Rules Governing Expansion And Contraction

The new guidance issued in 2003 purports to make it easier for successful schools to grow, permitting all schools to publish their own proposals to expand, and if they are rejected by SOCs, to appeal to the Schools Adjudicator. The guidance suggests that there should be a strong presumption in favour of the expansion of successful and popular schools. Any proposal whereby an existing school is to be enlarged so as to increase its capacity by 30 pupils and which, taken together with previous enlargements, will increase capacity by 25% or 200 pupils, whichever is the lesser, must be published. Decisions to allow a school to contract are again taken by the SOCs. Proposals for the removal of surplus places should be welcomed.

Rules Governing School Opening
The decision to open a new school is taken by the SOC and must go through a Statutory Proposal process. Currently, the rules state that there should only be support for provision of extra places where it is strongly supported by all parents in an area, would be demonstrably beneficial to local children and would not adversely affect other schools in that area. In considering proposals for new schools or the expansion of places, the SOC should take into account whether the proposal is going to meet particular demands in an area (e.g. for denominational or single sex education) and should balance those demands against their cost and the overall supply of places in an area. When considering changes of school category, the SOC is to remember that all types of school are equal and that foundation, community, voluntary aided or controlled are equal and that provision should not be made in favour of one over the other. The SOC also needs to take into account whether more places are needed as a result of population growth, the effects of surplus provision, whether diversity of provision would be enhanced and whether public money is used in an effective way. The SOC requires written confirmation that sufficient capital is available as well as recurrent funding and, in the case of early years provision proposals, there is an additional requirement to demonstrate that the opening has a specific function in combating social deprivation. These stipulations add up to a severe prohibition on opening a new school.

Rules Governing School Closure
Decisions are taken by local SOCs, whose decisions are final, with the only possible challenge being through judicial review. There should be a strong presumption against the closure of rural schools. Where a denominational representative is opposed to the closure of a school, an Adjudicator to the Committee should not take a decision that would affect the balance of denominational schooling in an area. When closing nursery years schools, SOCs can think about alternative provision from the private or voluntary sector, but only if they think the result will be a rise in standards. Eventually, in the case of

failure, closure is suggested as the most obvious course. Schools under special measures or subject to warnings under the School Standards and Frameworks Act of 1998 may become subject to a *Fresh Start* programme. If that is the case, then SOCs should be strongly disposed to approve closure of a school, and consider proposals for a replacement school in tandem with the closure proposal. If a school is under special measures, then the Secretary of State has the power to direct an LEA to close it, a decision that does not need to be passed by the SOC. In the last 4 years, 138 schools in special measures were closed when it was considered that better provision existed elsewhere, while 778 were 'cured'.

Consultation

The Secretary of State orders that proposal makers must consult all interested parties, including: any school that is the subject of proposals; any LEA concerned, especially those likely to be affected by cross border movement; other schools in the area that might be affected; parents and teachers, especially those at schools likely to be closed down as a result of a new opening; the governors of the school and the LEA where it is proposed to increase or reduce the school's standard number. There must be a statutory objection period of 2 months after which the SOC makes a statutory and unanimous decision to pass the proposals, reject them or demand that they be modified in accordance with objections. If the SOC is divided, the Secretary of State's Adjudicator steps in to make a decision.

Helping Self-help

There is an obvious paradox in the government acting to produce self-help from non-state actors. Hence, any recommendations for government action will necessarily be rather general in nature. All the same, there are three pointers for future policy:

1. The cycle of innovation

Ideas for solving problems at source have to start and be nurtured. This does not happen by chance – it may well require analysis, exploring the problem, analysing the causes, then shaping some options for change. It may also require time and expertise not often dedicated to the cause. Bounded experiments – such as many of those reported here, can be delivered with some focus of expertise and resource. The key, however, to execution and sustaining the result, even in only one local context, must be building resilience into the model, finding legitimate and robust leadership and commitment. Most importantly, and we believe lacking in today's systems, is the ability to self adjust and replicate at scale. This whole cycle has to be learned and developed itself at scale if community owned problem solving is to have accelerated benefits in the wider system.

2. The importance of leadership
In all the successful cases the leadership of individuals has been vital. Many different types of leaders emerge – but with the challenges described such leadership has to have a bias for action, and a perseverance to break through to new models of success. These leaders are everywhere in the system – the challenge is how to find, nurture and develop them.

3. Political commitment
If the system continues to respond to the short-term demands of insecure politicians or scandal-seeking media then we will continue to see public services responding to today's symptoms. Machinery and funding will stay short-term and will be divided amongst different agencies that myopically look at their own narrow measures. The government has to have the confidence to provide funding for the long term. Politicians in power at all levels must also be prepared to engage with all political colours on this quest.

Chapter Five
Mission-Driven Government

Sir Michael Bichard

Executive Summary

Reinventing Government now looks hopelessly optimistic,
looking back a decade later - public services are still marked by
a collective failure of leadership and a failure to focus on results
– the main problem is the civil service which remains averse
to risk and obsessed with process – leadership is not valued
enough and operational management ability is poor – the service
has avoided the necessary accountability and does not import
creative thinkers from outside - politicians have failed to realise
the importance of civil service reform – they need to make
much more use of private and not-for-profit providers as an
alternative source of policy advice – in fact this market is
diminishing and greater choice for citizens has been a casualty.

Targets are an important device but there have been too
many, they have often been about process rather than outcome
and very rarely addressed to the needs of clients – too often targets
have demoralised staff and produced perverse incentives –
targets should be more about distance travelled than destination
and they must be connected directly to service priorities – at
the moment this is an opportunity lost - the growth in audit
bureaucracy has been enormous and damaging – the NAO
and the PAC have not been modernised and the upshot is that
innovation is filtered out of the system – the disappointing
progress of e-government is a telling example.

If we are to liberate the talent of public servants we need
to define the mission and allow creative leadership to flourish –
that will revive the lost passion for reform that was stirred by

Reinventing Government – these leaders will focus their energies on service quality and will not be afraid of taking risks – improvement will depend on the rediscovery of creativity.

Introduction

I remember reading Osborne and Gaebler for the first time. I had recently left local government to run the Benefits Agency. I had a passion for public service reform. I still do. I believed that public services had failed too many ordinary people for far too long. Those people had been failed not by any lack of commitment on the part of public servants but by a collective failure of leadership, political and official. Most of all, they had been let down by the failure to provide a clear vision and a focus on results as they would be defined by citizens. In that context I thought that the chapter in *Reinventing Government on* "Mission-Driven Government" was too tame and I remember saying so to Ted Gaebler with rather less humility than he deserved.

At the time there were grounds for optimism in the UK. Next Step Agencies were – at their best – transforming the delivery of government services and providing a sense of pride and identity for staff which had for so long been lacking. And when that optimism was threatened by the passage of time, by a government in decline and by the vested interests of the mandarin class, the cavalry arrived in the form of a new administration committed to public service reform.

So why is it that now, a decade after publication, *Reinventing Government* looks hopelessly optimistic? Why is it that, after so much activity, investment, rhetoric and good intentions, too many ordinary people are still being failed? And – more important than any retrospection – just what can be done to re-ignite the flame and finally deliver mission-driven, results-oriented government?

The heart of the problem: the civil service

Central to these disappointments has been the failure to transform the heart of governance – the Civil Service. It is the Civil Service which prepares the legislative framework, devises the regulatory systems, sets the targets, decides when intervention is necessary and designs the incentives and sanctions. Unless the Civil Service is reformed there is precious little prospect of public sector reform becoming a reality. And yet in spite of the impressive rhetoric and the language of modernisation we still have a civil service that is risk averse, introspective, exclusive and process-centred. We have a service that continues to under-value the importance of leadership and management and lacks, at a senior level, people who know enough about operational management to be able to set and monitor sensible targets. We have a service which because of its structure, its training and the behaviour of its leaders is incapable of the creativity needed to solve the complex economic and social problems we face. We have a service, which has successfully avoided anything like the public accountability which it has imposed on other parts of the sector. And we have a service which has failed in most departments to import the fresh blood from outside which is needed to convert – in the words of Arie de Geus – the stagnant puddle into a fast flowing stream.

Why government has failed to grasp the nettle of civil service reform is an interesting question. Perhaps it is a collective political failure to understand the key part which the service plays in debilitating the rest of the sector; perhaps it is a fear on the part of ministers of being accused of political interference; perhaps it is a reluctance to cause ill feeling so close to home; perhaps senior ministers have just been seduced by the mandarins' skilled rhetoric and believe that modernisation is taking place. In spite of the efforts of a minority, it is not and will not without a more radical strategy.

One part of such a strategy should involve the more imaginative use of alternative providers – much talked about in the early days of this Government. These alternative providers might be in the private or the not-for-profit sector. They could offer services and products but equally they could offer alternative policy advice to that so often derided by ministers in private. They could bring new ideas and approaches and they could provide benchmarks to help measure the efficiency of the traditional providers. In reality, however, the talk of building market capacity has all but disappeared. New markets have not grown at a rate sufficient to encourage greater private sector investment. And the civil service has, because of its lack of management competence, managed those contracts that do exist in such a bureaucratic way that many companies are now persuaded that the game is not worth the candle. As a result a key requirement for improved public services – greater choice for the consumers – has failed to materialise. And the creative stimulus which competition provides has been lost. It is true that the private sector has on occasions failed by its performance to provide the evidence to justify further liberalisation in the face of union opposition. But public services have, until recently, received inadequate investment and been riddled with restrictive practices. Reform was never going to happen without some failures. It is a short-sighted lack of courage not to look beyond such setbacks to the longer-term benefits of a pluralistic provider base.

The rights and wrongs of targets
Osborne and Gaebler argued particularly strongly for results-oriented government, with output measures defining the performance an organisation was supposed to achieve. They argued for this as a way of freeing organisations and officials to use their creativity for the benefit of citizens. What we have seen instead in the UK is a diet of micro-targets set by officials who are intent on controlling the sector for their own purposes. In effect, the focus on results has been subtly used to centralise, prescribe and disempower rather than liberate. This is not to argue for a return to the unfettered professional freedom that produced such provider-dominated services in the past. Focus and accountability are prerequisites for effective governance. Targets are an important way of focusing energy and effort. Without them the commitment to service excellence, which the public sector has in abundance, will be wasted as public servants reach their own different conclusions about priorities and service levels.

But targets are so powerful that they can as easily do damage as deliver benefits. And that has often happened as we have seen them used by people who have little experience of operational delivery and little sensitivity of what is realistically achievable. So many targets have been set that it has been impossible to use them to focus attention on priorities (as Chief Executive of the Benefits Agency I was regularly given in excess of 150 targets).

Many of the targets have been about process rather than outcomes and, as a result, many of the outcomes have not been measurable. Evaluation has therefore been impossible. Too rarely have these targets been expressed in terms of client needs and even more rarely have clients – or even front line staff – been involved in designing or setting the targets. Effective targets are set to be stretching but achievable in the knowledge that unrealistic targets do not raise performance but merely demoralise staff. And that is what too often has happened. Targets can also distort behaviour as people use their ingenuity to achieve the measures by which they are judged. They need therefore to be reviewed regularly, frequently refreshed and properly audited. Rarely has that happened with the result that the media have been able to uncover too many embarrassing stories of targets being 'fiddled' for pay or bonus purposes.

We have also seen too many examples of targets being set solely at national level so that they mean little to the local providers who will ultimately dictate whether they are achieved or not. Targets need to cover all levels of delivery so that everyone knows just what their contribution to successful achievement needs to be. And often these targets, local and national, should be more about the distance travelled in performance rather than absolute levels. That is especially important if public service providers working in the most difficult areas or the most difficult schools are not to feel constantly undervalued as they appear regularly at the foot of league tables. That is one certain way to ensure that targets are not owned by staff and rarely in the recent past have targets been owned by those responsible for delivery. That lack of ownership has been exacerbated by the fact that, whereas Osborne and Gaebler saw a focus on outcome measures as a route to creativity and recognition, targets have been used to stifle creativity and focus attention on failures – especially when reinforced by inspection and assessment regimes equally preoccupied with identifying failure.

Above all targets should reflect service priorities. Often, however, there has been little relationship with key priorities and targets have been used to fudge the difficult decisions. To take but one example, the key question on benefit payments was whether the priority should be speed of payment (with the acceptance of some resultant errors) or accuracy (with consequently slower payments). But that tension was never resolved in the targets set which left payments staff unclear where to focus their efforts, confused about the priorities and feeling that they could only struggle to fail.

The way in which the perfectly sensible preoccupation of *Reinventing Government* with results has been distorted by this increasingly perverse use of targets is a classic case study of how damaging ideas and methodologies can be when they fall into the wrong hands – in this case inappropriately experienced senior managers. It also goes some way towards explaining why the vision of Osborne and Gaebler has not been realised. The tools of accountability need to be in the hands of people who know how to use them and who understand they are not solely there for the purposes of control.

Reinventing Government contended that rules make cowards of employees. Organisations driven by a mission, by contrast, are efficient, effective and have higher morale. Osborne and Gaebler suggested that budget and employment rules are the biggest constraint on missions. Both must be handled flexibly and rules are the enemy of flexibility. Organisations with missions should become obsessive about outcomes.

The growth and failings of the audit bureaucracy

Another important strand of the Osborne and Gaebler vision was deregulation – the need for fewer, better-targeted, contracts and more streamlined accountability. In reality we have seen an unprecedented growth in an audit bureaucracy which can involve one delivery agency struggling to cope with several different audit regimes, each of which requires the same information to be retained in different formats with each of the audit bodies demanding access to satisfy its own particular requirements at its own convenience. We may be told that, since 1999, the Regulatory Impact Unit based in the Cabinet Office has reviewed the revised regulations for public sector organisations but the experience of most will be the same as my own at the London Institute. The demands of Higher Education Funding Council, the Learning and Skills Council and government have increased and opportunities for sensible streamlining have so far been ignored often because they are inconvenient for one or other of the many regulators. In effect the people trying to deliver quality at the front line are crippled by the rigidity and arrogance of the centre. Service quality is sacrificed on the altar of bureaucracy.

Worse still has been the failure of the National Audit Office and the Public Accounts Committee to modernise and sharpen accountability in the way the Audit Commission has at least partially achieved. Instead of focusing on the quality of business management and policy development – and then focusing selectively on the most ineffective units – both have chosen instead to use resources randomly. They have selected issues which often win column inches but which do little to improve the quality of government. As a Permanent Secretary I rarely felt anyone - the Secretary of State aside - was much interested in how well managed was my department.

Worse, the way in which the various accountability regimes have developed has encouraged managers to follow the traditional approaches because they are then more likely to receive praise from largely conservative auditors and inspectors. Thus, the innovation and experiment so essential to the Osborne and Gaebler vision has been systematically filtered out of the system. After all, why try something different when you can be assured of high grades in inspections by doing things in the same safe old way? Why take risks to transform outcomes when the balance of incentives and sanctions is weighted so negatively?

A case study in retarded innovation: E-services
Government spokesmen point to the 63% of services which were enabled at the end of 2002. But the reality is that the usage of e.services is depressingly low. In fact a recent government outline study from Taylor Matson Sofres found that while the number of users accessing e.government services worldwide had increased from 15 to 30% over the past twelve months, the UK was the second worst (to Japan) with only a 13% adoption of e.government services. In addition, few government departments have achieved the organisational

change needed to make it transformational; insufficient
e-funding has reached the frontline services (notably local
government) and politicians appear to have been discouraged
by the perceived 'high profile' failures. Modernisation and
e-government are inextricably linked but momentum has been
lost and Osborne and Gaebler revisited would surely identify
the creative use of IT at a local level as key to reinventing
government in the future. After all, the ultimate purpose
of reinventing government is to provide services, which are
accessible to all; personalised; relevant to a highly diverse
community and transparent. It is difficult to see how this can
be achieved without the effective deployment of IT but the
record to date hardly offers grounds for optimism.

Looking back, in summary, the great tragedy of the past
decade has been the way in which successive governments'
reform strategies have been lost in the detail of implementation
or undermined by the machine. Most recently the Prime
Minister's perfectly respectable strategy of standards, devolution,
flexibility and choice has, as I have described, been lost in a fog
of targets, accountability, control and centralisation.

How to reinvent government

But what of the future? Have the lessons been learned? I fear
not. We have been told that we can look forward to a 'major'
and historic programme on efficiency! With (my words) more
targets and more control, lower overheads, greater efficiency
and a stronger focus on customers. This all sounds depressingly
familiar and will founder as surely as previous reform
programmes unless it addresses the key question raised by
Reinventing Government. And that key question is this: how
can we liberate the energy and talent of public servants to deliver
world-class services and policies within a well-defined, widely
accepted vision for public services (such as the Prime Minister's)?

To answer that question we surely need to develop a wholly
different set of questions. We need to concentrate on:

- Defining the mission
- Describing the outcomes
- Building creativity

- Improving leadership and
- Growing the change capacity.

But if the legacy of Osborne and Gaebler is to be fulfilled the most important of these is creativity and leadership – the need to rediscover the passion, the initiative and the innovation that will alone transform public services (see Chapter 7 in this volume in which Keith Ruddle looks at reinventing operational management and Chapter 8 in which Steve Bundred considers the nature of reinvented political leadership).

Leadership and risk

We need to develop a new breed of creative leaders who believe that it is possible to enhance creativity and who believe that creativity is not a 'given'. They will be people who have invested effort in retaining an open and fresh approach to life and work. They will be skilled at encouraging new ideas and will treat sympathetically ideas that are brought to them. They will understand that the best leaders are not necessarily the people who make quick decisions but often those who suspend judgement long enough to allow innovative thinking to be assessed. They will probably shun hierarchies and status, knowing that these prevent the free-flow of ideas that fuel creativity. These creative leaders will be working hard at making connections inside their organisation and beyond because they know that creativity often derives from making the unexpected links. Perhaps above all these leaders will have the ability to build energy in their organisations.

Looking back, in summary, the great tragedy of the past decade has been the way in which successive governments' reform strategies have been lost in the detail of implementation or undermined by the machine.

As much as anything else *Reinventing Government* was a testimony to passion and energy. It spoke about public services with belief and excitement and that is what we have lost. The creative leaders will help us rediscover it. They will show that they value more the people who innovate and produce ideas rather than those who elegantly critique others. They will have the determination to make a reality of Osborne and Gaebler's desire to eliminate activities that add no value – the meetings no one wants and the excessively elaborate reports. And they will do that because they know that such activities consume energy that should go towards providing better services. Equally, they will target excessive friction between the parts of government – local and national – which make organisations dysfunctional and show by their actions that playing politics, managing upwards and watching your back are unacceptable distractions from service quality. They will be better too at developing climates of trust within which people feel able to manage the risks that go with creativity. And they will know how to handle the well-managed risk that goes wrong.

One of the problems of the legacy of *Reinventing Government* is that too many people took from it that public service reform was solely a question of improving the quality of management. But that was never going to resolve the problems our communities face – nor was it, to be fair, what the authors said. To resolve complex, fast-changing social problems requires above all creativity – which is not the same as intellect. Re-hashing yesterday's policies will not be sufficient to reduce today's yet alone tomorrow's problems. But the past decade has seen an obsession with management and little focus on policy development, analysis and creativity in spite of the transparently poor quality of these processes. The next decade should be rededicated to reinventing government, by rediscovering creativity. That alone will deliver the original promise of Osborne and Gaebler's ideas and provide the public services our people deserve.

Chapter Six
Reinventing Inspection

David Bell

Executive Summary

Inspection serves three broad purposes: to police national standards, to identify failure and to make a contribution to institutional improvement – it has a long history but has grown significantly recently – Ofsted is a case study of inspection in action and of how it can be reinvented - Ofsted was invented in 1992 to inspect schools, since when its remit has broadened to local education authorities, colleges, childcare and children's services – it is, crucially, an independent body which reports directly not to ministers but to parents – the criteria used for forming judgements are published and its models of school effectiveness have not been seriously challenged - parents and teachers at all levels have access to data on their schools – this has led to 1,100 failing schools being identified in the last decade and remedial action mandated – Ofsted was also instrumental in the national literacy and numeracy strategy, intervention in poor performing councils and inadequate teacher training – of course the cost and the methods employed by Ofsted have attracted critics - inspection is not an exact science but 90% of schools surveyed agreed their inspection was fair. It is now time to reinvent inspection making more use of self-evaluation and the published performance data – inspection need not be so comprehensive, it can be a short assessment of fundamental performance, at a maximum interval of three years, given with very short notice – reports would be more frequent but the overall burden lessened.

Inspection has to contribute even more than it does to

school improvement – some cases little progress has been made in 'coasting' schools – there is also a danger that a culture of compliance is created in which schools adapt to the dictates of inspection – reducing the notice period will make this less likely – this needs to be supplemented by a new attitude from central government which has to resist micro-management and remove bureaucratic obstacles.

There is a danger that loosening the grip of the inspectors could be seen as giving way to professional interests and we cannot return to a system of complete self-evaluation – in any case self-evaluation has been strongly influenced by Ofsted – the kind of data available to policy makers will change and it will be important to ensure that the new regime is still fit for identifying the likely outbreak of failure – this should be eminently possible.

Introduction

Inspection serves three broad purposes: to ensure that minimum national standards are reached; to identify failure; and to stimulate institutional improvement. The inspection of public services has a long and distinguished history. The first inspectors of schools were appointed in 1839 with inspectors of constabulary being appointed just over 25 years later. But in the last seven years the work of inspectorates has expanded considerably. Now, it is estimated that around £0.5 billion per year is spent on public sector inspection and that does not include the costs that fall on those who are on the receiving end of this activity.

The growth of inspection, though, has lately come under increasing scrutiny. From within government, the Public Sector Productivity Panel, the Office for Public Service Reform and a joint Prime Minister's Delivery Unit and H.M. Treasury review of public services have assessed the contribution made by inspection to date. Those being inspected have regularly made their views known. Even those who were not opposed in principle to inspection began to question the costs of compliance: far from energising local management, it was said, over-inspection meant that staff spent their time worrying about what inspectors wanted and, consequently, were less willing to take risks.

Thus the time is right to consider the role of inspection as the next phase of public sector reform comes under scrutiny. The Office for Standards in Education (Ofsted) makes an interesting case study. Through it can be seen the origins of modern inspection, the impact that this has had and the capacity for reinvention to serve a new purpose.

Ofsted: the best known of inspectorates

Ofsted was the brainchild of the Conservative government in the early 1990s. Despite becoming one of the best known brand names in the public sector, the name 'Ofsted' did not appear in the 1992 Education Act. The rather wooden title, 'Office of Her Majesty's Chief Inspector', soon gave way to the much more populist 'Ofsted' with its highly distinctive chalk-on-blackboard logo.

Over the years since 1992, Ofsted became so well known that it spawned a noun, 'to have an Ofsted' and the rather vulgar verb, 'to be Ofsted-ed'. More importantly, it became successive governments' inspectorate of choice as it saw its responsibilities expanded to encompass more than just the inspection of schools. Local education authorities, colleges and childcare were all added to Ofsted's inspection and regulatory remit. Most recently, Ofsted has been given the lead responsibility for the inspection of children's services in local authorities and beyond.

Through Her Majesty's Inspectors (HMI), the full time, permanent staff of Ofsted, there are regular discussions (formal and informal) with officials from the Department for Education & Skills (DfES), other government departments and agencies, such as the Qualifications and Curriculum Authority (QCA), awarding bodies, the national strategies, or the Teacher Training Agency (TTA) and professional associations in their subject.

In addition to this broad remit, the work of Ofsted has always rested on four key principles:

1. Ofsted has constitutional independence under the Crown and Parliament that requires inspection and reporting to be fair, rigorous and impartial.

2. Ofsted gives priority to its extensive statutory duties: to

regulate and inspect childcare, and to inspect schools, colleges and teacher education, the work of local education authorities, and a range of other provision.

3. Ofsted reports directly and openly to the public: to parents and others who are clients of those who provide education and care.

4. Ofsted ensures that all of its reporting and advice to government, those who work in education and care, and the public, is authoritatively rooted in robust evidence.

Each of these principles, when first established, was ground-breaking and they continue to shape the debate about the role of inspectorates in the public sector. For example, the inde-pendence of Ofsted is more than just symbolic. It is neither part of a 'parent' Whitehall department nor a non-departmental public body, unlike almost every other inspectorate. Rather, as a non-ministerial government department, headed by a Crown appointee, it has an authority and independence which is well understood in the wider world. Although part of the Whitehall machinery and subject to Treasury budget disciplines and remit letters from ministers, Her Majesty's Chief Inspector has an independence to speak out in an unfettered manner. Such a position has not always been comfortable for politicians as successive chief inspectors have been prepared to criticise cherished policies that have failed to deliver what was promised. Equally, Ofsted's reporting responsibilities represented a radical departure for any regulator or inspectorate. Rather then reporting directly to ministers or, in the case of Her Majesty's Inspectors of Schools prior to the creation of Ofsted, reporting very infrequently on individual institutions, Ofsted ensured that parents received regular reports on their child's school. Combined with the publication of test and examination results, this led to the English education system becoming the most open and transparent in the world.

The creation of Ofsted brought into the public domain the criteria inspectors used in the course of their work. Up until then, most inspectorates made highly subjective judgements. There were no common criteria and even quality descriptors on a standardised scale only emerged towards the end of the

1980s. By way of contrast, Ofsted's methodology became public property. Again, this changed the terms of debate and now no inspectorate would even attempt to make judgements simply based on a form of professional connoisseurship.

The models of school and college effectiveness that are represented in Ofsted's inspection instruments have not been seriously challenged. Indeed they have been so successful and universal that some have accused Ofsted, though its work, of hijacking the educational debate. Inspection frameworks have sought to accommodate change in a considered way, by not responding in a knee-jerk fashion to every new initiative, but by providing timely and carefully considered responses to major developments, such as the evaluation of leadership, performance management and the introduction of the foundation stage curriculum.

Osborne and Gaebler relegated what they had to say about inspection to an appendix on the art of performance measurement. In a sense, inspection fills in for the parts of government that have yet to be re-invented. Inspection, along with the panoply of targets and centrally-set performance measures, has been one of the principal means by which UK governments have sought to improve public services.

The impact of inspection

It is unarguable that Ofsted's impact has been profound over the past decade. Ofsted has ensured that every school in England has been inspected at least twice. Parents have been provided with crucial, and previously unavailable, information about the performance of all schools and not just those attended by their own children. Potential teachers can compare the quality of training providers before deciding where to apply, and know that their training will be quality assured. Career teachers can compare their schools with others and get an insight into the quality, standards and challenges of schools they may wish to work in.

Crucially too, every headteacher, teacher and governor, has access to an independent diagnosis of the strengths and weaknesses of their own school. This in turn leads to actions for improvement. Ofsted's approach to the identification of failing schools, over 1100 in ten years, has been the most dramatic example of inspection being used to drive up improvement in public services, but not the only one. The Ofsted survey of reading standards in London local education authorities had a direct impact on the creation of the national literacy and numeracy strategies. Its work in local education authorities stimulated government intervention in the worst performing councils. And most recently, Ofsted's spotlight on the inadequacies of teacher training in further education led to a radical rethink on the part of ministers. The transparency of information provided by Ofsted, whilst not always welcomed by professionals, has set a benchmark that is unlikely ever to be lowered, in education or any other part of the public sector. Of course, Ofsted has not been without its critics. Teaching unions have, at times, criticised what they see as its punitive approach and have rejected anything that looks like the 'naming and shaming' of underperformers. Members of Parliament often return to the cost of Ofsted, not least in relation to the bureaucratic overhead it is said to generate as schools prepare for and respond to inspection. Researchers criticise Ofsted's methodology, with some arguing that it is fundamentally flawed. So, it is worth saying more about the nature of inspection and what it attempts to do.

What is inspection?
The process of inspection which evolved slowly between 1830 and 1988 and rapidly thereafter, is best summed up by a former Senior Chief Inspector of Schools, Sheila Brown: 'The basic principle of inspection has always been close observation exercised with an open mind by persons with appropriate experience and a framework of relevant principles.'

The inspection system today remains true to this guiding definition. However, there are those who would argue that inspectors' observations are inconsistent and unreliable. And even if these were more reliable, some critics assert that aspects of learning such as the progress that pupils make and what they learn in lessons are not amenable to observation because they are not reflected in specifiable behaviours. In addition, critics would argue that the contribution made by schools and teachers to pupils' achievements cannot be distinguished from other factors.

Inspectors though take great care to draw upon data from a variety of sources. So, for example when judging the quality of teaching and learning, inspectors do not presume that they can see inside pupils' heads. Rather, they combine their direct observations with skilful questioning and analysis of pupils' work. Taken together with performance data, they can come to a rounded judgement. Indeed, so they must. Parents and other observers would look askance if it were suggested that no possible judgments could be made about the quality of education in a school without months or even years of scientific research. Schools, in the main, themselves recognise what inspectors say about them. Almost 90% of the 3,000 of the schools who respond to Ofsted's inspection survey each year attest that their recent inspection findings were 'fair and accurate'. Inspection does not claim to be a science, but neither is it an undisciplined enquiry.

There are elements of inspection that are indeed subjective because inspection relies on professional judgement. In that respect, it is distinct from financial audit. However, the criteria and guidance Ofsted provides are intended to constrain subjectivity and ensure reliability and consistency. When this has been tested from time to time, it is found that most inspectors are working within acceptable competence limits.

The availability of data and the desirability of basing inspection on a schools' self-evaluation means that the theory of inspection is based partially on a notion of falsifiability. The argument being: 'The school says it is like this and the indicators tend to agree.' The best way of confirming this is to test the hypothesis by looking for exceptions to it, although to take this too far is to be accused of finding fault. In doing this, Ofsted has to take particular note of unusually effective practice as well as diagnosing where things could be improved.

Inspectors are less concerned with the various behaviours exhibited in the process of teaching, and whether these are the 'right' ones, than with the effect that the teaching is having on the pupils. So, the most challenging part of inspection is to determine whether pupils are learning as much as they should or could. There are many ways of testing this, but one is actually to examine the pupils about their understanding of the work they are doing. If they find it well within their grasp and easily respond when set new problems or applications of what they have done, then it is possible their achievement is not high enough.

Reinventing inspection

But of course as public services move on, so it is important that their inspection and regulation evolves too. Recent cross-government reviews of the work of inspectorates and regulators have co-incided with radical thinking from within Ofsted about the future of inspection. The new approach to inspection that Ofsted is now advocating could and should influence the work of other inspectorates. 'Reinventing inspection' is now the most pressing task in the years ahead.

Education has improved over the past decade. Data is now much more widely available, increasingly at the level of the individual pupil. This is particularly significant because it is now possible to track the progress that individual and groups of pupils make, beyond the headline indicators of test and examination results. In itself, this provides a good basis for rethinking inspection. Ofsted's data suggests that self-evaluation has become better as school leaders become more sharply focused on the strengths and weaknesses of their own institutions. Thus, inspection need not accumulate the wealth of detail at the level of the individual institution as it did in its earlier incarnations. Greater reliance can be placed on the published and publicly available performance data, standing alongside institutional self-evaluation.

Ofsted's data suggests that self-evaluation has become better as school leaders become more sharply focused on the strengths and weaknesses of their own institutions. Thus, inspection need not accumulate the wealth of detail at the level of the individual institution as it did in its earlier incarnations.

This has two consequences for the way inspection is carried out. In the first place, the overall weight can decrease as there is much less need to encompass everything during a 'routine' inspection. For example, it makes less sense to look at every subject of the curriculum when data is available from other sources. The second consequence is that inspection can focus more sharply on the quality of self-evaluation. Inspectors can judge how far the reality of the school conforms with the self-evaluation. Where there is a close co-incidence, this is likely to be a good indicator of future improvement. Where the self-assessment and the inspection seriously diverge, then this raises significant questions about the quality of leadership and may trigger further intervention.

In essence then, a reinvented system of inspection will entail a short and focused review of the fundamentals of a school's performance and systems at an expected maximum interval of three years, integrated with school self-evaluation and improvement planning. The new model of inspection has to focus sharply on the key elements of a school's work, in particular those originally laid down in the legislation that created Ofsted; standards achieved by pupils, the quality of education, the spiritual, moral, social and cultural development and leadership and management. Such inspections, for which very short notice would be given, would, across a six year period require about half the total number of inspection days currently allocated to six-yearly school inspections. Reports would be provided more frequently to parents and others and the whole process would be likely to stimulate more rapid improvements through more frequent contacts with schools, leading to clear recommendations for action.

School improvement
But it is also essential that a reinvented approach to inspection has a more direct impact on improvement. That is not to suggest that inspection has failed to have such an effect over the past ten years. Successive annual reports from chief inspectors reveal a steady and encouraging improvement in what children and young people know, understand and can do; in the quality of teaching; and in the effectiveness of school leadership. But it would be wrong for the system to become complacent when

many other indicators suggest either a lack of progress or stagnation in performance. Inspectors provide an independent account of how well a school is doing and identify recommendations for improvement. Subsequent inspections monitor the progress that has been made. In the case of the weakest schools, the contribution to improvement has been more dramatic with the system of special measures triggering action at school, local authority and national levels. Inspectors too are more strongly involved as schools in special measures are subject to regular monitoring.

Equally though, inspection may not have provided sufficient challenge to some schools. Ofsted's experience of starting to inspect some schools for a third time suggests that in too many cases the same deficiencies are being reported as leaders, governors and local education authorities fail to grapple with fundamental problems.

There is also another factor to consider. There is no doubt that the first inspection of any institution has a strong element of compliance. In other words, acceptable levels of performance in teaching, learning and management were identified when Ofsted published its first framework for the inspection of schools. Despite, the criticism that schools were only 'doing what Ofsted wanted', this could be robustly dealt with on the grounds that Ofsted criteria described minimum levels of acceptable performance. So, if schools were improving to that minimum, that in itself was an important step forward. The danger over time though is that this creates something of a compliance culture, an effect that is often commented on wherever inspectorates are active. For some institutions, failure to 'comply' is catastrophic as has been demonstrated in the case of schools that require special measures for not providing an acceptable standard of education to their pupils. But if compliance has been secured in the majority of schools, then inspection has to adapt to ensure that its work adds value beyond this basic level of assurance.

So, in the majority of schools more can be done to ensure that inspection contributes to improvement. Increasing the frequency will ensure that recommendations are acted upon and schools do not stagnate. Focusing relentlessly on the quality of leadership ensures that the key drivers are in place to bring about further improvements. Dramatically reducing the period of notice will ensure that schools are seen they are and not as they would like to be seen. That, of course, has the benefit of removing much of the unnecessary pre-inspection preparation that is currently associated with a longer period of notice. Fundamentally though, changes to the system of inspection only make sense if they are seen as part of a new relationship with schools. Government needs to move away from a relationship that is marked by micro-management and cumbersome bureaucracy to one that unlocks the energies of school leaders. This is a lesson that is more generally applicable across the public sector and one which all departments, inspectorates and regulators need to understand.

The dangers of reinventing inspection

To move inspection forward in the way described above is not unproblematic and there are a number of issues that need to be considered. Firstly, and perhaps most seriously, is the new relationship with schools and the reinvention of inspection a surrender to professional interests? For some, any reducing of the 'weight' of inspection is to move too far in the direction of what suits the interests of teachers and thus denies parents and the wider public access to the kind of rich data they have had in the past. So, it is important that a reinvented inspection system maintains rigour and independence and is seen to be doing so. Ofsted's experience with weaker schools suggests that when inspectors maintain regular contact, the rate of improvement can be rapid. The same has been shown to be true as Ofsted now revisits colleges that demonstrate significant weaknesses on their first inspection. For all schools, six years between inspections is likely to be too long and a new model enables both a lighter touch in the best schools and more frequent intervention in the weakest.

There is an irony in that others might see the reinvention of inspection as a means of tightening the screw. Shorter inspections at minimal notice and gathering less evidence on which to base judgements could be seen as a punitive approach. Again rigour and independence are crucial. Rigour to ensure that the evidence is sufficient on which to base judgements and independence to demonstrate that inspection is not merely a tool of government to 'get tough' with teachers.

The move to shorter and more frequent inspection may also disappoint those who have previously complained about the weight of inspection. School leaders will not have every aspect of their provision inspected and not all teachers will be inspected, particularly in secondary schools. To that extent, there will be a trade off but one that should reinforce the view that institutional self-review should be at the heart of improvement, and not 'left to the inspectors'.

A second critique could be that reinvention does not go far enough in the direction of institutional self-evaluation, peer assessment, community evaluation and the like. Some would argue that acceptance of these approaches would truly represent a new relationship with schools.

There is little difficulty with this as a principle. But the inspection system only grew out of a situation in which local authority practice of monitoring and evaluating their schools was extremely variable and largely non-existent. The majority of schools were reluctant to introduce rigorous approaches to appraisal; performance management was nowhere in sight; and schools for the first time were, under local management, responsible for significant amounts of money.

Equally though, it would be fair to say that the inspection system has evolved to keep pace with the growing competence of schools in some of these matters. Indeed there is much evidence that the methods designed and used by Ofsted have been widely adopted by schools, particularly in the area of self-evaluation. Thus it is reasonable now, but certainly was not a few years ago, to place greater reliance on schools' self-evaluation and to take a much greater account of this in planning inspections. Where the inspectors' evidence is consistent with the school's own analysis then this is likely to be the sign of a healthy institution. Where self-evaluation is actually self-delusion then it is only right that this triggers additional intervention.

A third potential difficulty for the new approach is one for policy makers. The kind of evidence that they now have about the education system as a whole will not be the same as they are likely to have in the future. Presently, the chief inspector's annual report is able to comment on every dimension of schools' work because, simply, every subject and aspect is included in every inspection. This will not be the case in the future. But increased frequency will provide new, and potentially more powerful information although particular themes e.g. the quality of history or science teaching may need to be pursued via additional studies and surveys.

A fourth concern relates to the continuing high stakes nature of inspection. If inspection visits are to be shorter, does this not make it more questionable to describe schools as 'failing' and requiring special measures? Arguably, however, a new inspection system might lead to clearer judgements because there is less clutter in the inspection framework. In addition, the framework for inspection will contain clearer and easier to understand criteria. Coupled with the increasing availability of data and the centrality of school self evaluation, then inspectors will have all the information they require.

Conclusion

Inspectors might be permitted a wry smile as they reflect on that not unknown tendency of governments to 'run against themselves'. After all, the expansion of inspection work over the past few years has been driven by ministers as they have sought to pull an additional lever in their quest to improve public services. A change in the mood music from central government should not divert attention from all that the various inspectorates have achieved in the last seven years. Despite these successes, inspection should not be the same seven years from now. It needs to be lighter and faster while retaining its efficacy in identifying failing performance. Self-evaluation will become more important rather than less and, as government explores new routes for public service reform, it will be important to retain our stress on the value that intelligent inspection can bring.

Chapter Seven
Reinventing Leadership

Keith Ruddle

Executive Summary

Leadership is a crucial ingredient in good performance which was almost wholly absent from *Reinventing Government* – leadership in the public sector today is very complex and requires different approaches, notably to work in partnership with very many types of body – the challenge for government is to create the space for leaders to lead - there are more than five million employees in more than 25,000 organisations in the public sector and leadership occurs at all levels.

Leadership can be characterised as entrepreneurial (leading innovation), organisational (managing collaboration) or institutional (sustaining change) – leaders need to communicate a clear sense of direction and then have the confidence to allow their teams to manage the process – the hierarchical model of leadership is often no longer appropriate – it is more accurate to imagine the leader of the future as a key connection point in a network - good leadership producing a culture change can be seen at work in four examples: The Reading Creative Education scheme, the South West Regional Development Agency, the Employment Service and the Defence Aviation Repair Agency.

There have been a great many leadership initiatives in recent times but public services are still not attracting and keeping the best leaders – we need to reinvent political leadership, to rebuild trust and to be wiser in our use of central control, not least by promoting better leadership in

1 Osbourne and Gaebler
Reinventing Government,
page 136.

government – most examples of good practice involve clear
political leaders who then permit their officials to do their
work – there are plenty of examples in local government of this
favourable balance – the audit and inspection regime needs to
be reformed to stop the diminution of trust that is currently
taking place.

The leaders of the future will be less hierarchical and
more collegiate than in the past - they will need to inspire their
people and then have the courage to trust their teams – this is
required by political leaders every bit as much as operational
leaders - although some slow progress has been made, much
remains to do.

Introduction

How did Northumbria Police increase its crime detection
rate for six years in a row and keep its area one of the safest
in the country, despite the major cities it protects? Why
does the Thomas Telford School in Shropshire achieve the
Sportsmark Gold Award, the Charter Mark, Investors in
People and Investors in Careers accreditation and why
do 100% of its pupils achieve five GCSEs at grades A-C?
And how does Tameside Borough Council achieve four
beacon awards, eight consecutive years of Britain in Bloom
awards, and become the first council to e-enable 100%
of its services?

Good leadership is almost always critical to success –
never more so than in times of change. Yet despite its importance,
the matter did not make a chapter in Osborne & Gaelber's
original manifesto for *Reinventing Government* - only a
sentence or two to confirm that; 'nothing is more important
that leadership…. Typically the leader is a mayor, city manager,
governor or president but leadership can take many forms.
In some places a group of leaders has acted together. At times
leaders push government from the outside, at other times
they are internal department heads'[1]. *Reinventing Government*
left this important issue hanging - what kind of leaders
would be needed? Clearly leaders would be needed to
embrace philosophies such as mission-driven, decentralised,
results-oriented, and enterprising government. But what
kind of people were required and did they exist?

Osborne and Gaebler said almost nothing about leadership although the importance of good leadership was taken for granted throughout the book. The need for effective leadership is so vital in public services that it requires a section in itself, hence the two essays devoted to it in this volume.

The elusive idea of leadership

Leadership is one of those things that people often think they know when they see it. The very concept can be elusive but, in the context of the public sector we need to bear in mind three issues:

1. the complexity of the problems which face today's public sector leaders

2. a recognition that leadership requires different characteristics in different contexts

3. a challenge for government: to allow successful leaders the freedom to develop.

Complex problems, leadership complex

Where do we need to look for leaders who will change the public sector for the better? Once upon a time, our thoughts might have been exclusively focused at the very pinnacle of the public sector. This is no longer true. The public sector is one of the most – if not *the* most - complex organisations in the economy. It includes agencies (large and small), non-departmental bodies, health trusts, schools, fire-brigades, to name but a few. There are over five million employees and more than 25,000 public sector organisations. Focusing on the top of the senior civil service, therefore, will lead us to miss the many levels at which real influence and change can be generated. It is simply not the case today that, if only we could find 300 budding Napoleons or Jack Welchs, we could reinvent the UK public services. There is always a great deal of discussion about this elite cadre of the top 200-300: about their pay, their rewards, and whether more should be brought from the private sector.

But transforming leadership in the public sector is much more complicated than this. Indeed, solving the riddle of just *who* is leading the public sector and how can be difficult. In the course of the recent study of leadership conducted by the

2 PIU, *Strengthening Leadership in the Public Sector,* UK Cabinet Office, 2001.

Performance and Innovation Unit (PIU) in the Cabinet Office, David Clarke, formerly Chief Executive of York City Council asked a pertinent question: "Who is the key leader of the education system in a city such as York? Is it:

• Tony Blair as Prime Minister

• David Blunkett as Secretary of State

• Michael Bichard as Permanent Secretary

• Rod Hills as Leader of the Council

• Janet Looker as Executive member for Education

• David Clarke the Chief Executive

• Michael Peters the Director of Education   or

• a collective of heads who run the schools?"[2]

Any action on leadership needs to be at all these levels. The leaders themselves need to understand they are part of this complex structure.

Different contexts, different traits
So what does successful leadership look and feel like in today's public services? How do different types of leadership contribute and what can we learn from them? We might suggest three broad categories that appear particularly relevant to a changing public service of leadership:

• Entrepreneurial
The entrepreneurial leader instigates and leads innovation and performance delivery. This style has recently been given more prominence by some of the national initiatives to identify and share best practice.

• Organisational
The organisational leader is a master of collaboration, skilled in communicating, coaching, connecting and bringing diverse interests together to deliver new services and solve new problems.

• Institutional
The institutional leader champions the overall purpose, and transforms and sustains change, a very common requirement in public services.

Entrepreneurial leaders

In recent years, organisations such as the Audit Commission, the NHS Modernisation Agency and the Improvement Development Agency (IDeA) have been in the forefront of nurturing a style of leadership that attempts to foster local innovation. Some examples of this approach were recently highlighted in Charles Leadbeater's book for the IDeA, *The Man in the Caravan*[3].

In the PIU study for the Cabinet Office, the team took the approach of finding over 200 public service leaders and asking them to tell their own stories of what good leadership felt like. All the individuals were different - many did not display the outward persona often associated with charismatic leaders – but all had achieved success within a complex system. From this analysis we drew the following sets of characteristics:

3 Charles Leadbetter, *The Man in the Caravan*, Improvement and Development Agency 2003.

Leaders with inner strengths
- are reflective and self aware
- know that they cannot lead alone
- ignore ridicule
- have courageous patience
- take time
- treat short term as if it was long term
- are consistent
- desire to be included and fear being left out
- are gladly accountable
- hold themselves accountable for the whole
- fail – and learn from failure.

Leaders with outer strengths
- draw on multiple perspectives
- believe in us more than we do ourselves
- know how to create trusting relationships
- demonstrate integrity
- can dissent when needed
- use feedback
- rely on our commitment and creativity
- know we are only motivated by meaningful work
- know how to support and appreciate
- state what really counts
- give an account of what they've done.

Organisational leaders

The modern public sector cannot work without partnerships. This means individual leaders working with colleagues in their own organisations but also working across the usual borders. The net result is a collective form of leadership. The following case study demonstrate this aspect of leadership in action:

Case study 1: South West Regional Development Agency (RDA)

The new RDAs needed to establish relationships with a very wide range of businesses, voluntary groups, and public bodies. In the South West, the Chair, Sir Michael Lickiss, and the Chief Executive, Jill Barrow created a new culture for the Agency, working on local relationships with over 4,000 meetings, conferences and 60 road shows and joining up with many different government departments.

Many other institutional arrangements are now in place to foster collective leadership including Local Strategic Partnerships, Youth Offending Teams, and joint home care initiatives to name but three. All these examples, where successful, see leaders able to align strategies and resources across boundaries without being dragged down into the mire of consultation and consensus.

So, leadership in the public services now implies partnership with others. But what characterises successful collective leadership? We can identify two sets of qualities:

in achieving collective cohesion leaders...

• focus on defining and reinforcing identity

• lead and champion change and the future

• use participative processes for intractable problems

• create possibility rather than fix problems

• make organisations safe for 'mavericks, deviants and mermaids'

• have minimum standards and act when breached

• connect to daily reality of staff and public

• use political demands as catalysts not as an end in itself in working with other organisations leaders...

- push control down

- value multiple perspectives

- use different models of partnerships depending on the circumstances (cooperative, collaborative, co-evolution)

- seek strong partners and build fair trades between them

- recognise that intermediaries can distort

- know they cannot do it on their own

- understand that relationships and connections are core business

- know outcomes are too important to be left to measures alone.

Institutional leaders

The third type of leadership involves transforming major delivery arms of the public sector. The two case studies of the Employment Service (1997 - 2000) and the Defence Aviation Repair Agency (1998 - 2001) demonstrate how institutional leadership can inspire reinvention and then sustain change.

Case study 2: The Employment Service (ES)

With around 35,000 staff, the Employment Service was one of the largest executive agencies. In 1997 it ran old-style and often cramped job centres. It was largely seen as 'administering the job seekers scheme'. The new government chose to use the ES to deliver the New Deal. The three years to 2000 saw radical changes, a shift in culture and values, major new technology, new ways of 'treating customers' and a step change in service levels. After 2000 a programme of reform continued. It included the merger with the Benefits Agency to form the new Job Centre Plus.

The key institutional change was a gradual shift from command and control at the top of the agency towards more strategic thinking at the centre about the whole system. This required leaders who could think differently at the centre and regional leaders who could negotiate effectively with politicians and the chief executive officers of local businesses.

For the Chief Executive of the Agency and a regional director, the change entailed a shift from an organisation governed by rules to one governed by mission. For the Chief Executive this meant personally being visible, painting a picture of the future, being outward looking and using all channels to communicate with 35,000 people. For a local job centre manager, the change was about nurturing and developing personal leadership through the issue of new challenges to solve and being stretched but encouraged by institutional leaders.

Case study 3: The Defence Aviation Repair Agency (DARA)
DARA emerged as a 7,000 strong support agency for the armed services out of the 1998 strategic defence review which amalgamated Naval and Airforce repairs under one Chief Executive. Its immediate mission was to reduce output cost by 20% by 2005 but also provide the lean support defined by the Ministry of Defence. Radical changes in culture and processes were necessary to achieve this. Rapid response support meant working in major partnerships and alliances. The first three years saw significant reductions in lead times and response. There were four important aspects to the required leadership:

* a clear focus on vision, values and strategy
* strong accountability whilst empowering team leaders
* belief in managers taking ownership of problems and solving them
* motivating and inspiring people.

The change process saw a heavy investment in leadership development for the top 50 managers, 360-degree evaluation and feedback, extensive communication methods including fast-track briefings for all employees. The support given by ministers from central government was also very important.

New organisational models for leadership
In a traditional organisational chart, the leader is easy to spot. As managers rise to the top of the tree they get to allocate bigger

and bigger packages of resource. But, as Sumantra Ghoshal and Chris Bartlett pointed out,[4] this hierarchical model of leadership is no longer an appropriate picture. Many public leaders are better envisaged leading the way with new ideas, meeting new customer needs and innovating. This kind of leader provides the immediate drive for people in the field. In a fast changing world it is this kind of leader who is best able to define new services and link up with others to deliver the stated objectives. Thus, the job centre manager, the class room teacher and department head, the health clinical director and manager are all at the leading edge of the new leadership.

The public service leaders of tomorrow may be better imagined at the centre of a network. They will be attempting to link resources and strategies both within and across organisational boundaries. They will also provide support and coaching to their teams providing the service. In organisations where best practice and ideas come from within, the role of transferring knowledge across the system is vital. Here department heads, technical specialists, function heads and geographic heads will be the principal leaders.

This is not to say, of course, that the leader at the top of the tree is a thing of the past, only that their *modus operandi* may have to alter. As we saw in the Agency examples above, the prime role for this institutional leader is to champion the purpose and values of the organisation (or indeed the system), challenge assumptions, inspire commitment and also provide the context in which change and success can take place. It is this leadership role which perhaps needs most attention in the public services and which leads us to the question of what politicians might do to help.

4 Sumantra Ghoshal and Chris Bartlett, "Beyond the Russian Doll Management Model" Navigating Change, HBS Press 1998.

The public service leaders of tomorrow may be better imagined at the centre of a network. They will be attempting to link resources and strategies both within and across organisational boundaries.

	From	To	Key roles and traits
Operating Managers	Operational Implementers	Aggressive Entrepreneurs	• Front line motivator • Energy & drive • Innovation & growth
Senior Managers	Administritive Controllers	Developmental Coaches	• Supporting, parenting coaching • Linking knowledge and practices • Relationships and reconciliation
Top team	Resource allocators	Institutional leaders	• Championing purpose and values • Challenging assumptions • Inspiring confidence and commitment

Adapted from: Bartlett & Goshal 1998

The role for government in reinventing leadership

Before suggesting what government might do next it is worth pausing to assess the progress that has been made in reinventing public sector leadership in recent years. There has certainly been no shortage of initiatives. The Cabinet Office and the Centre for Management and Policy Studies have focused again on central leadership training in the national civil service. The national school heads leadership programme encourages head teachers to join peer groups and learn from each other. The National Health Service (NHS) leadership programmes - and indeed much of the approach of the NHS Modernisation Agency - are now focused on self improvement. Agency Chief Executive David Fillingham described it as feeling like 'the three year point on a 10 year journey'. In local government, the recent Leadership Development Commission brought together employers, the IDeA and central government. All present agreed that a national leadership strategy should be developed to meet the challenges in local government. The IDeA's own programmes of leadership renewal try to spread knowledge and practice from local government and other sectors.

All this activity this should not distract us from the reality of how far there is yet to travel. In its own report, the Cabinet Office itself noted that:

• public services were not attracting or keeping the best leaders

• that leadership development, while plentiful, was not necessarily effective nor sufficiently cross-sector

- that leaders were too often not given the 'freedom to lead' or the support systems

- that there was little shared understanding across the services of the real qualities of effective leadership.

Lessons for the next Government
So there is still an awful lot to do. Serious progress on this key issue will require an explicit recognition that good leadership throughout the public sector can flourish only with a renewed emphasis on training and development and on changing the very *conditions* in which public sector leaders operate. There are four ingredients:

1. the need to reinvent political leadership
2. the reinvention of trust alongside accountability
3. more wisdom in the use of central control
4. new leadership capability at the centre of government.

The first condition is nothing short of a reinvention of political leadership (this theme is discussed a greater length by Steve Bundred in Chapter Eight of this volume). Examples of great political leadership are still too thin on the ground. There remain too many politicians who think short term, act as individuals, thrive on factions and opposition, and fail to understand effective collaboration and change. There are now real role models for the better, and there needs to be real effort to find new and younger people prepared to learn this new profession.

Threaded through the examples in this essay lies the conundrum of political leadership and its influence in the system. Osborne and Gaebler's examples of good leadership were usually political. Political leadership and accountability create a context different from that of private organisations. Political leaders establish values. Officials then interpret these underlying values in their context - and in the light of their ethos of public service. Politicians also remain ultimately accountable for public service delivery, even though intermediaries (such as agency chief executives) can put great distance between politicians and front line delivery. Public accountability comes in very different ways: governance, democratic control and accountability to other public bodies. Public services are also largely funded by taxpayers, following political and parliamentary decisions. This leads to an inevitable tendency for politicians to monitor and intervene.

The key tasks for the reinvented political leader must be to set clear objectives and create the climate in which officials and organisations have the freedom, motivation, legitimacy and resources to lead in action. The separation of politicians and officials is crucial. Most examples of bad practice involve a breach of this separation: the poll tax twists and turns, over-centralising the health service with detailed monitoring, inter-departmental turf battles and rows between ministers and agency heads. The most well-known examples are the dispute between Derek Lewis and Michael Howard and, more recently, the resignation of Beverley Hughes. Conversely, where policy has been successful, the national ministers have set a clear course and permitted it to be implemented: this can be said of the New Deal, the programme to create combined benefits and employment Job Centres (originally the ONE project) and of Sure Start. The national numeracy and literacy initiative also saw strong championing from David Blunkett with the recognition that a sharp centralist approach on a well-defined objective could get professional support in practice. The most successful Local Education Authorities (LEAs) are those in which politicians were decisive and then refused to interfere in implementation.

In local government the new arrangements of cabinet responsibility and 'professionalising' the role of elected members were all greeted with some caution but many stories are now emerging of clear political leadership. Examples include Sandy Bruce Lockhart's vision in Kent of 'helping people to live independent lives', Blackburn's Bill Taylor striving for unitary status and Northumberland's Jim Wright in social services combating disadvantage and social exclusion.

The second condition is a reinvention of trust alongside accountability. In her Recent Reith lectures Baroness Onora O'Neill pointed out very effectively that the notion of detailed targets and measures reported to the centre undermines both accountability and trust. Politicians who are insecure often seek more monitoring and regulation 'to restore public trust in the system'[5]. Such moves however, inevitably take trust away from the relationship between local and institutional leader. Output and performance measures are important; but the audit and inspection regime almost certainly needs more careful calibration.

5 Onora O'Neill, *A Question of Trust*, Reith Lectures 2000.

The third condition, not unrelated to the second, is the issue of wisdom in the use of central control. Local freedom to lead is often available in theory but undermined in practice. Recent examples might be Primary Care Trusts in the NHS (often set with boundaries too small to allow real capacity to commission), past approaches of Ofsted inspection in schools (alienating teachers through over-critical styles), the Home Office 'finger-wagging' at police for not imposing curfews on children and over zealous use of performance indicators in the Best Value programmes (nearly 200 indicators often based on inputs rather than outcomes).

Finally, there is the question of new leaders at the centre of government. This point is elaborated by Sir Michael Bichard in Chapter Five. While much has been made of reforms of the top civil service, reinvention requires a new kind of adaptive leadership that can grasp and work across the whole complex system.

Conclusion

Leadership was a notable omission by Osborne and Gaebler. It cannot go missing from the reinvention we still need for public services. The leaders of the future will not be like those of the past – they will need to be less hierarchical and more collegiate. They will need to inspire their people with a picture of where they are heading together. They will then need to have the courage to step aside to allow their teams to implement their vision in practice. This requirement is every bit as necessary in political leaders as it is in operational leadership and, although some slow progress has been made, we still have a long way to travel.

Chapter Eight
Reinventing Political
Leadership

Steve Bundred

Executive Summary

Leadership matters, as many excellent local leaders are demonstrating – a series of service failures were all characterised by poor leadership – well-run local authorities generally provide good services – auditing involves political judgement but the requirements of political leadership differ from place to place.

Users of public services are now more demanding than ever before – they expect choice over their services and once this is granted there can be no going back – even though councils are improving, public satisfaction is declining – voters always say that environmental services matter most to them but local politicians cannot divert more resources to them because education and social services are greater national priorities – protecting the vulnerable, in defiance of majority opinion, is a perfectly proper function of national government.

Council leaders now have to work as much through influence as through executive power – they are also charged with objectives, such as reducing health inequalities, which go beyond the basic provision of a service – accountability can often be murky in partnerships, especially where there are pooled budgets – but there are examples of innovation, from administrations of all political colours, where local governments are working with other sectors.

Political leaders also have to settle conflicts over scarce resources such as school places – they require legitimacy in order to be able to do this – this comes from the ballot box, from clear decision-making processes and from the provision of good services – this is the way that politicians will build trust – they have to respect other organisations and build the capacity of their community – the more diverse the community the more difficult this is - local politicians now need to think about prevention rather than cure and about negotiating the maze of funding possibilities now that a much greater proportion of local authority funding is hypothecated for specific purposes - councils also have to contend with structural change which shows no sign of abating - political leaders always set the tone of their area's service provision even where they choose to allow officers to take the lead – the political complexion of a council leads to distinct priorities.

The common traits of good political leaders are that they set the values and priorities, they adapt to crises, they motivate staff, they plan and monitor progress and they take calculated risks - leadership can be learned, both formally through study and by example – competition imitation has led to clusters of excellent councils – but good leaders are still a minority and there is insufficient commitment from local politicians and parties to improving – the absence of good leadership produces apathy rather than pressure from voters for improvement – politicians need to embrace better leadership before it is too late - local government needs a new sense of purpose – national political parties have some responsibility for this and better ways need to be found to transfer good practice across authorities – local government needs to take itself more seriously – it needs to establish leadership colleges to make leadership a strength in depth – otherwise this period will come to be seen as an opportunity lost.

Introduction

When Osborne and Gaebler wrote their seminal *Reinventing Government* in 1992 they had surprisingly little to say about leadership. The transformation taking place in the public sector that the book was written to describe and applaud was the work of a new wave of ambitious and entrepreneurial leaders within American public services. And if nothing else, a key lesson of Osborne and Gaebler's book was that leadership matters.

1 *Patterns for Improvement*, Audit Commission, 2003.

You don't have to agree with Rudy Giuliani to acknowledge the impact he had on New York. Nor do you have to support former mayor Pasqual Maragall to be impressed by the changes he brought about in Barcelona. Closer to home, there is no need to refer back to Chamberlain's Birmingham to find local politicians who have transformed their communities. Examples of council leaders who are making a real difference can be found everywhere. Sir Bill Taylor in Blackburn with Darwen, Sir Sandy Bruce Lockhart in Kent, and Mike Storey in Liverpool are just a few of those whose achievements have gained national attention over recent years.

One of the clear messages to emerge from the Audit Commission's comprehensive performance assessment (CPA) of single tier authorities and county councils in England was that strong leadership, and the clarity of purpose associated with it, is central to success.

'Councils perform well when they have political leadership that focuses on change and continuous improvement; and makes – and sticks to – tough decisions, even in politically sensitive areas[1].'

Too often, the explanation for serious failure in public services of all kinds lies in a failure of leadership. It was an implosion of political leadership that gave rise to the crises in Liverpool in the 1980s and Hackney in the 1990s. The Audit Commission's report, *Corporate Governance* (2003), which drew on the learning from the death of Victoria Climbie, the scandal of child deaths at Bristol Hospital and the Alder Hey organ retention scandal, found a failure of leadership in each case. As the Audit Commission has learned to understand and acknowledge the importance of political leadership, and to develop an ability to assess it within English local government, it has felt able to justify less interference in the detail of service management. Well run local authorities generally deliver good local services and, where not yet doing so, will normally identify performance weaknesses and address them. This has permitted the Commission to adopt a more risk-based approach, with local authorities judged to be excellent overall through CPA receiving no inspection of services.

CPA uniquely involves judgements about political leadership. But some such judgements are easier to reach than others. Few would disagree that local politicians who bully their officers, refuse to take difficult decisions, or are unaware of how their authority compares with others, are unlikely to be producing good outcomes for their communities. In contrast, the political leadership that inspired Manchester City Council following the devastation of its city centre by an IRA bomb in 1996 can only be admired. But the kind of leadership that has been responsible for the transformation of Manchester, and is witnessed in the recent renaissance of several of our other major city centres, may not be the same as that needed in a rural authority facing no immediate crisis and with no party having overall political control. The challenges that leaders face differ according to local circumstances. But more importantly, they are changing over time; and changes over the last decade have made local political leadership a more demanding task now than ever before.

Osborne and Gaebler said almost nothing about political leadership although the importance of good leadership was taken for granted throughout the book. The need for effective leadership is so vital in public services that it requires a section in itself, hence the two essays devoted to it in this volume.

Greater expectations and falling satisfaction

Some of these changes were predictable. As Osborne and Gaebler anticipated, users of public services no longer see themselves as claimants, tenants, passengers, or patients – but as customers. The public demands more of local government. It is less deferential to authority and less tolerant of under-performance. And significantly, it is no longer enough that a local authority should provide good quality services. Users now also expect a degree of choice over how services are delivered, or who the provider should be. The days when couples were content to be married in grim Town Hall registry offices are gone; they now expect to be able to choose from among a number of more attractive venues licensed to hold such ceremonies. And gone too are the days of councils being able to dictate to those living in its properties how hot their dwellings should be or what colour their door should be painted. With the advent of direct payments, those receiving social care packages now exercise a degree of choice over the packages they receive. And, once having obtained this power to take such decisions themselves, there is no possibility that users of public services will ever give it up. Instead, they will demand an ability to exercise choice over more areas of public service. So it is now part of the job of local political leadership to satisfy these demands.

However, while local government is getting better at responding to users in this way, public satisfaction with local councils is at the same time declining. The evidence provided by analysis of performance indicators and year-on-year comparison of CPA results clearly shows that council services are improving. Local authorities now listen more and are more likely to respond. But they are not noticeably rewarded by increased trust and confidence in them – because in local government, there are limits to how responsive they can be to a purely local agenda. Successive opinion surveys have shown that the key driver of satisfaction with local councils is the performance of environmental services. When asked what issues are most important to them, voters always place street cleansing, waste collection and street lighting alongside crime and anti-social behaviour at the top of their list. And when asked about their satisfaction with individual local authority services and with their local authority as a whole, the strongest correlation is invariably that between the performance of environmental services and overall satisfaction.

Successive opinion surveys have shown that the key driver of satisfaction with local councils is the performance of environmental services. When asked what issues are most important to them, voters always place street cleansing, waste collection and street lighting alongside crime and anti-social behaviour at the top of their list.

So, an authority intent on improving local satisfaction would divert resources towards improving the performance of its environmental services. But in doing so, it might be neglecting national policy priorities, for which it could be penalised. Modern local authority leaders are caught between conflicting national and local demands. National policy, perfectly properly, dictates that education is the major priority, as reflected in national funding decisions. Second only to education as a national policy priority is social care, especially the care of vulnerable children. But education and children's services are seldom likely to be top priorities for local voters. Children do not have a vote; the majority of households do not contain children of school age and most children are not in contact with social services.

It is entirely reasonable for central government to determine that children's services should be a priority for local authorities. This is not because local government is merely an agency of central government, although this is now more true than most people in local government feel comfortable about. Nor is it because national taxpayers contribute most of the money spent by local authorities; this is a product of history rather than principle. But instead, because it is the job of government to protect the vulnerable and if protecting minorities involves overriding the wishes of a majority then it is sometimes the responsibility of government to do so – even if this creates real difficulties for local political leaders.

Working in partnership

Council leaders can no longer confine their ambitions to things for which they are directly responsible. They can no longer expect to achieve their objectives solely through their own actions. Attracting inward investment, reducing health inequalities and reducing crime and the fear of it are all aims that go beyond the narrow remit of improving the quality of the services delivered by the local authority. All of these are to be found within many local authority corporate plans and local public service agreements (LPSAs).

Effective leadership is therefore now characterised by creativity and pragmatism. In the terms used by Osborne and Gaebler, successful councils now steer more than they row;

they solve problems by leveraging the marketplace rather than simply creating public programmes. There is a much reduced degree of political dogma within local government now than in the 1980s and early 1990s, but no less political idealism. Political beliefs and values are still driving what leaders do but they must now draw upon a wider range of skills to achieve their aims. In particular, they are expected to achieve many of their most important objectives through no more than the exercise of influence. This is a constant activity, which may usefully be contrasted with the previous ability of council leaders to make decisions and then forget about them, in the sure knowledge that they would be implemented by competent officers.

Influence may occasionally be exercised within partnership structures that have a formal, sometimes even a statutory, framework. But, even in statutory partnerships, accountabilities are often confused, and the leadership challenge made correspondingly complex. This is especially true when the partnership involves the pooling of budgets or joint appointments to key posts. The partnership landscape is also constantly changing. Within the Innovation Forum of councils recognised as excellent through CPA, thought is now being given to how to extend the partnership approach into other spheres. Kent County Council, for example, is leading a debate about ways of reducing welfare dependency by joint working with the Benefits Agency. Strategic partnerships between local government and the private sector are also now commonplace. They have been central to what authorities as diverse as Labour controlled Blackburn with Darwen, Conservative Westminster City Council, and Liberal Democrat Liverpool have begun to achieve. So councils now need high level procurement and enterprise skills. They need the ability to take important strategic decisions about whether to make or buy and they need to be able to handle different types of relationships with external bodies as partners, contractors, voluntary organisations, or a combination of all three.

Seven challenges for political leaders

Local political leadership is not just about the delivery of council services. Councils have many different functions, of which delivering services is increasingly becoming secondary to other roles. Amongst the other functions of good local leadership, the following seven stand out:

(i) settling conflicts
(ii) acquiring legitimacy
(iii) building community capacity
(iv) upholding non-governmental organisations
(v) prevention rather than cure
(vi) negotiating the funding maze
(vii) structural change.

Indeed, perhaps the most important function of local government is not about service delivery at all, but is instead about the reconciliation of conflict in civil society. Local authorities are regulators, mediators and arbitrators. They referee disputes between neighbours, for example in their role as planning authorities. And they enforce the law, for example in relation to food safety or child protection. They are also responsible for the rationing of scarce public goods – a hugely important part of their role. Public housing is rationed by way of allocation policies; places in desirable schools are rationed by way of admissions policies; social care services are rationed by way of needs assessments; and road space is rationed through parking controls. To fulfil all these roles effectively, councillors require legitimacy and trust. The ballot box provides some of this legitimacy. But elections alone are not enough.

Among the other ways in which local authorities acquire legitimacy and trust are the transparency and consistency of their decision making processes. People are more inclined to accept decisions they don't like if they understand the reasons for them and if they feel that anyone else in their position would have been treated in the same way. But more important is the quality of the leadership that authorities provide to their community. Councils and councillors gain legitimacy and win trust by the extent to which they are perceived to understand the needs of their communities (recognising that in each locality there will be many different communities), and to be shaping services in response to the views expressed by local service users and taxpayers. They must be seen to be speaking on behalf of their communities, articulating the concerns of residents and, most importantly, mobilising resources to address these concerns.

It is through community leadership that politicians build trust, and building trust is one of the toughest tasks they face. Council leaders must explain how the needs of their communities differ from those of others, and ensure that local community planning is distinctive in capturing this local flavour. As they do so, the best leaders demonstrate the added value that politicians bring to local government. They are able to view their authorities from the perspective of local residents and taxpayers, and they have an authority as leaders of their communities, and as advocates on behalf of local people, that could not be equalled by appointed officials.

This is true even when recognising, as they must, that politicians are not the only legitimate voice of community interests. The best leaders work with and respect the views of others – which includes respecting the autonomy of community groups that may be wholly dependent on the financial support of the council. In doing so, they also build social capital and promote active citizenship by developing the skills of local community groups. And the more diverse the community, the more challenging is this task. The language of meeting the special needs of minority communities has given way to recognition that these communities have rights, interests and legitimate demands, not merely needs. Responding to these is part of the normal functions of local government and cannot be accomplished through a modern form of paternalism.

It is no longer sufficient to talk of responding to unmet needs. Effective local politicians now need to prevent rather than cure. When the arcane employment practices within fire and rescue services were exposed to public gaze by an industrial dispute in 2003, it was the existence of targets and performance indicators that focus only on reaction to failure which proved most shocking. Modernising the fire service will involve re-focusing it on prevention – just as crime reduction is now the central objective of many Local Strategic Partnerships (LSPs).

In comparison with their counterparts a decade ago, local authorities also now face a more complex array of funding streams. Winning and allocating resources is therefore a significant function of local political leadership. Despite a Government commitment to reduce the level of ring-fenced grants, and some recent evidence of progress, the proportion of local authority funding that is hypothecated to specific purposes is much greater than it was a decade ago, with the number of ring-fenced grants requiring audit certification having increased from 100 in 1988/89 to 190 in 2003/04. And perhaps more importantly, a large element of the block grant distributed to local government is for all practical purposes hypothecated by ministerial announcements about school funding that effectively pre-empt local decisions about resources allocation.

Finally, structural change also poses a challenge to political leaders. Councils are still coming to terms with changes in political management involving the separation of executive and scrutiny functions and the introduction of elected mayors. LSPs and LPSAs have created new mechanisms for accountability and target setting. Housing management is moving beyond the direct remit of local authorities as new arms-length management organisations take root. Adult social services are now being delivered jointly with the NHS, often in new trusts led by NHS professionals. New children's trusts are leading to the dissolution of separate education and social services departments. New regional authorities are on the brink of being established in the North of England. In the counties, significant changes may be in prospect to the remit of the strategic planning function and there is a continuing debate about whether housing benefit and council tax collection should continue to be a function of lower tier authorities, or even a local government function at all.

The traits of political leaders
But despite the extent of change over recent years in the challenges that local authority leaders face, some key elements of the leadership role are universal:

(i) leaders set the values and priorities
(ii) leaders adapt to crises
(iii) leaders motivate staff
(iv) leaders plan and monitor progress
(v) leaders take calculated risks.

What political leaders do, above all else, is to provide clarity of purpose. Effective leaders make it clear what the priorities are, show focus and tenacity in achieving them, and by so doing capture

2 Quoted in *The Man in the Caravan and other stories*, Charles Leadbeater, IDeA 2003.

the imagination of, and inspire action by, others. To command credibility, the objectives that leaders set must be ambitious and communicated in ways that are easy to understand and that make the vision appear not merely attractive, but also achievable.

In local government, where political and managerial leadership are distinct but ill-defined, the importance of this cannot be over-stated; nor should its complexity be under-estimated. Some well-run local authorities are successful because their politicians have chosen to allow competent officers to direct the council's affairs. The success of others derives from being more transparently driven by their politicians. Examples of the former are typically found in authorities where there is no one party in overall control. As Steven Parnaby, the Conservative Leader of East Riding Council, once put it: 'the first job of politicians is not to screw things up'[2].

But in both cases, the underlying values are necessarily those of councillors. When voters exercise the choices they make at the ballot box, they mostly do so without reference to detailed manifestos, but instead rely on their understanding of what the parties broadly stand for. And in general, they are justified in doing so. Councils run by all three major parties deliver high quality services. But there are observable differences in the priorities attached by different parties at local level to matters such as local tax levels, social inequalities, devolution and community empowerment, and development control.

Nowhere is this more apparent than in central London where neighbouring authorities, providing equally good services and recognised as being excellent in CPA, such as Conservative Wandsworth and Labour Hammersmith and Fulham, nevertheless have clearly distinct values, reflecting the politics of the ruling party. The same is true of Conservative Westminster and Labour Camden, both of which have been winners of the *Local Government Chronicle* (LGC) Council of the Year award in recent years.

Case study: Birmingham

After suffering huge employment losses in the early 1980s, as its traditional manufacturing industries became obsolete and disappeared, Birmingham's leaders recognised a need to make the city a more desirable location for inward investment and to develop and diversify the skills of the local workforce. So Birmingham embarked on a regeneration programme embracing the building of new leisure, shopping and cultural facilities (making impressive use of its canal-side), while also investing heavily in education. It formed new links with its universities and it greatly improved the performance of its schools to better equip local young people for employment in the industries that the city was soon attracting. In 1998, in recognition of these achievements, Birmingham was named by *Local Government Chronicle* as Council of the Year.

The Birmingham example shows the effect of good leadership in a crisis. In rural areas in 2002 many councils faced more sudden crises, caused firstly by an outbreak of foot and mouth disease and then by severe flooding. The leadership traits displayed in responding to these crises had much in common. Adaptability is part of the common thread, but more fundamental is the connection between the leadership and the communities they lead.

Leaders also motivate. The carefully prepared speeches in the mode of Churchill's wartime broadcasts are now a less common means of doing so than quiet words of encouragement; but more important than words, are actions. Effective leaders celebrate success and marginalise opposition. A few years ago, an Audit Commission inspection team visiting a local authority observed a particularly good example of customer care by staff on the authority's reception desk. They casually mentioned this

The best leaders know how their services are performing and insist on regularly receiving high quality, easily intelligible performance management data to enable them to challenge the managers of the relevant service areas.

in a conversation with the Leader, who promptly visited the reception area to thank the staff personally on behalf of the individual they had helped. At the same authority, members of the public were annually invited to nominate staff for customer care awards, while examples of poor customer care often resulted in compensation being paid to the recipient of the poor service.

Leaders also plan, enable and monitor progress. They navigate, identify waypoints by which progress can be measured, anticipate possible changes of course and prepare contingency plans to cope with unforeseen events. Often, they may also manage external relationships as part of this role. They allocate resources, and in so doing accept an obligation to ensure that the resources available are adequate to meet the demands placed upon them. Where progress monitoring suggests that the original plan is insufficiently ambitious or unlikely to be realised, they will review and adjust the plan accordingly. And at the conclusion of the planning period, they assess the extent to which the desired outcomes have been realised. The best leaders know how their services are performing and insist on regularly receiving high quality, easily intelligible performance management data to enable them to challenge the managers of the relevant service areas. Rudy Giuliani's weekly meetings with New York police captains about the crime figures in each of the city's police precincts have become a model that is now paralleled in many English local authorities. For example, the Audit Commission found, as part of its corporate assessment for CPA in 2002, that

'Wigan has a strong performance driven culture and has a number of systems in place or under development to manage performance. It has few weaknesses in this area. The council monitors performance indicators well, has established appraisal systems and undertakes compliance audits to ensure these systems are adhered to.'

But it remains striking how many local politicians, when asked which services are causing them most concern, still struggle to answer. It is no coincidence that the authorities found by CPA, or the Audit Commission's corporate governance inspections, to be failing their communities, were frequently led by politicians in denial about their performance. The difference is that the best local leaders typically display a degree of competitive behaviour, constructively channelled into ambitions for their communities and the authorities they lead. They are conscious of how good their services are and how they compare with others and they aim to do better than comparable authorities on all counts.

The best leaders are also courageous. They take calculated risks and they behave with integrity, even when this is likely to undermine their support. Again, there are many examples of this. The introduction of congestion charging in central London was a calculated gamble, as was Gateshead's investment in public art. The closure of a library, or a rural school or bus service invariably involves a degree of political risk. And so too does a decision to raise taxes, even to fund a popular service such as street cleansing, or alternatively to cut services and grants to voluntary organisations in order to bring local taxes down to a more reasonable level. But effective leaders are willing to take such risks.

Leadership development
Courage is a characteristic, not a skill or an attitude. Leadership, as we have seen, is in contrast a combination of characteristics, skills, attitudes and behaviours. It follows that much of what distinguishes the best local leaders are not innate qualities, but skills and behaviours that can be learned. Good authorities recognise this by demonstrating their commitment to being learning organisations, both collectively and individually. Their leaders reinforce this culture by participating in learning activities themselves. A few do so through formal development activities, such as university MPA or MBA schemes, or shorter courses such as university diplomas and the IDeA's Leadership Academy. Others participate in peer reviews and take trouble to find out what similar organisations are doing; they attend conferences and seminars; they read the articles that appear in the trade press and challenge their officers about ideas they have picked up from them; and they encourage senior officers to gain national positions within professional bodies. Competitive behaviours in successful local authorities are demonstrated not by relationships within them, but by the desire of the council as a whole to learn from and surpass the

best their neighbours can achieve. It is perhaps for this reason that when the first CPA results were published in December 2002, they showed clusters of excellent authorities in the North East and in inner London. Plausibly, peer pressure, arising from comparison with their neighbours, was driving the leaders of those authorities and contributing to their success.

But such leaders are not in the majority. While there are some examples of outstanding local leadership, too much of it is still not adequate to the more complex environment and the more difficult challenges councils now face. In recent years, failures of leadership in Walsall, Hull and elsewhere have prompted parts of Whitehall to see local government as a problem in need of a radical solution. So proposals to transfer more local services to central control, school funding currently being the most favoured suggestion, are much in vogue. Yet there are also voices arguing for movement in the opposite direction – for greater devolution of responsibility and more local discretion. Those who advocate change in the direction of a new localism also recognise the importance of political leadership but believe that the best way of nurturing political talent is to give it more freedom. So from both perspectives, the quality of local political leadership, and the extent to which it can be relied upon or developed, is a key element of the terms of debate.

However, there does not seem to be a strong commitment among local politicians to development activities. The IDeA's Leadership Academy, despite the high regard in which it is held, has barely scratched the surface of local government's leadership cadre. No political party has model standing orders for their local authority groups requiring councillors to extend their skills or making advancement to leadership positions conditional on doing so. And in some political groups there is a degree of opposition to formal skills development on the grounds that this is a managerial agenda which fails to appreciate the local accountability of councillors through the ballot box. So there is very little pressure from the culture of local government for a stronger focus on leadership development, and none at all from the electorate. Voters will often recognise good leadership when they see it, but its absence does not result in demands for improvement – more frequently it leads to apathy and disillusionment with politics altogether. But as we have seen, the political leadership of public services matters. The real challenge, therefore, is whether local government collectively, and politicians individually, are willing to embrace the need for leadership development before it is too late.

Conclusion

Local government needs to re-invent itself, to establish a new sense of purpose and relevance in the eyes of local electors and those who use and pay for public services. This requires a better quality of leadership than that generally present today, but not better than that currently to be found in the best local authorities. This is not simply a matter of incentives, financial or otherwise, aimed at attracting more talented individuals into local politics. The need is for cultural change, for which political parties at national level must accept some responsibility. Councils, and those who serve on them, need to become more outward looking and more self-aware. We need to find new and better ways of promoting innovation and transferring knowledge between local authorities. We need to recognise that local government is not just a collection of autonomous authorities, each different from the next, but also an economic sector employing nearly 10% of the UK workforce. We need to acknowledge that despite their differences, local authorities also have much in common. In doing so, we might begin to question, for example, why it is that Manchester United FC has its own satellite TV channel, but local government does not – or even why it is that politics programmes on terrestrial channels only show interest in local government when the focus is on council tax increases. And we might then start to draw comparisons with other European countries in which many local politicians are also seriously engaged, and heavily influential, at the national level.

All of this requires that local government should take itself more seriously, should stop behaving as a victim and apologising for its deficiencies, and should instead recognise its strengths and build on them. At present, the quality of political leadership is only a strength in a minority of authorities, and even in those there is often not strength in depth. It will not become a strength of local government as a whole without something resembling the leadership colleges that are to be found in other sectors. The danger, therefore, is that without a stronger all round commitment to the development of political leadership, the few dynamic, forward thinking local politicians that can currently be found within local government will come to be seen as an aberration. If this happens, commentators looking back on this period ten years hence may come to see it as an opportunity lost.

Chapter Nine
Reinventing Reform

Greg Wilkinson

Executive Summary
The basis of *Reinventing Government* was a twin belief in
enterprising management and the use of markets – there is
a critique of this vision now under way which needs to be
resisted – the original set of ideas needs to be revisited
and supplemented.

There have been changes to the structure of markets in
public services and to both demand and supply – the purchaser-
provider split could be extended by differentiating funding
towards the least well-off – a split between commissioning and
providing has improved prisons, is changing the nature of
social housing, could give new purpose to LEAs and could help
improve policing – government could allow greater fluidity and
dynamism in the supply of public services – school brands
could emerge in which a successful management team takes over
less successful provision – the same could happen in fostering
and adoption services and the collection of local taxes – schools
should be encouraged to see themselves as purchasers of the
best education every bit as much as a provider – this will help
liberate the excellent managerial talent that is currently isolated
within pockets of the public sector – good performance would
spread more rapidly and poor performance would be addressed
earlier – these reforms would require regulatory reform, the
design of incentives, cultural change and new methods of procurement – the local populace could be given a bigger say in
who provides their services.

Choice and convenience are bringing important and welcome changes to health care – it should be possible to extend this approach to other sectors – for example people should be given a guarantee of how long it will take to have a benefit processed and should be permitted to move to another provider if this limit is exceeded – customisation of services should also be extended, notably in schools where pupils could take a curriculum that suits them personally, at a pace that is appropriate to them – a school could become a kind of educational clearing house – these changes will require contestability between providers, good information, support to users and inscribing the right of citizens to change provider, sometimes underpinned by a voucher.

Management should be undertaken at the level of the operational unit, not the national service – government should stay out of the managerial process as far as possible – it especially needs to rid itself of the mindset that imposes new national programmes on services – there are two potential exceptions to this: information technology (IT) and personnel – IT has not transformed government services in the way it has transformed business practice – the implementation of the Gershon Efficiency Review and the NHS IT Modernisation programme have the potential to allow more effective use of IT in government - in the field of personnel, remuneration packages need to offer incentives and rewards for good performance – and it should be easier to get rid of poor performers – fixed-term contracts might be an appropriate mechanism for the police and the civil service, for example – salaries for high performers should be increased markedly and the barriers to entry pulled down by allowing no prejudice against non-professionals running public services.

Performance measurement is very important to reinvented public services but we still do not have a resilient measure of public value – such a measure will combine user satisfaction, wider social benefits, trust and economy and efficiency in providing services – the model of shareholder value can inform the design of a model of public value – this approach does have its limitations but it would allow us to make indicative comparisons of performance – it could help address the plethora of existing measures and increase the level of understanding of and engagement in public services – public services involve special relationships between users, providers and citizens and the principle of mutuality is important, particularly where effective change requires a shift in the behaviour of individuals – policing in some cities in the US, education in Birmingham and the work of Healthy Living Centres in the UK, have all, in their different ways, used the principle of mutuality to beneficial effect – this could be extended into local governance at the level of the neighbourhood.

All services would benefit from the principles set out in this essay - policing may need a combination of top-down reform and an approach rooted in mutuality – education would benefit from a reformed and extended purchaser-provider split and more contestability – in health a lot of good work is being done but there is further scope to give patients access to adequate expertise, to customise service provision to meet individual preferences and to help people change detrimental behaviour – the challenge for the civil service is to allow market mechanisms to decentralise power away from them – reforms should not lead to the end of audit and inspection but they would become a lighter presence – in the end reform has to be a political process if it is to succeed – change should not be left to technocrats.

Introduction

The ten principles of *Reinventing Government* encapsulated a more enterprising approach by both politicians and officials. The foundations of this new paradigm were a belief in markets and a readiness to apply principles of management to public services:

- The belief in markets generated attempts to increase competition and contestability on the supply side, stimulated either through the purchasing decisions of government or through the boosting of user choice

- The belief in management led to the importing of a series of concepts from commercial organisations – including decentralisation, deregulation, mission statements, performance measurement and management – to change the relationship between the centre of government and the operating units responsible for service delivery, and to improve the performance of those units.

We are at a critical juncture in this argument. As the essays in this volume have shown, government has yet to be fully reinvented in this country. And yet there is a powerful body of opinion around that would turn back such reinvention as has occurred. This alternative conception of service improvement is based on increasing budgets, dismantling reform programmes and accountability mechanisms, trusting professionals and providers to do a good job and opposing any significant involvement of private companies in public-service delivery on the grounds that the need to make profits will always be at the expense of levels and quality of service.

This critique needs to be resisted. The 'reinventing government' paradigm is not exhausted: there is still a great deal of scope for making public services in the UK more market-driven and better managed; and these are effective means of addressing the problems that those services face. But Osborne & Gaebler's principles will not be sufficient to meet the challenges that public services will face over the coming period. Their insights need to be:

- Refreshed, to reflect the insights that have emerged over the last decade into how markets might be used to improve the performance of public services and into what constitutes effective management and organisation of enterprises in any sector;

- Supplemented, to address the two key gaps in the book's framework: the lack of any model of value underpinning public services (and the ways in which their performance is measured and managed), and the lack of appreciation of the special character of the relationships between citizens and public services, and the opportunities that this 'special relationship' creates for efficient and effective service delivery; and

- Targeted with greater precision, to ensure that the right package of reforms is developed for each public service – while the goals of excellence and equity are universal across the public sector, there is no single recipe that can be applied uniformly to achieve these goals in each and every part. The skill required in reformers is less that of engineering and more of cooking: the ingredients of a reform package need to be selected and combined with skill and imagination to deliver the right results for individual services and institutions.

Such a 'reinvention' of *Reinventing Government* has the

potential to create the basis for a new programme of reform. It is helpful to consider the elements of such a programme under four headings:

- **Markets** – reforms aimed at making greater use of market mechanisms, choice and contestability

- **Management** – reforms aimed the ways in which public services are managed

- **Measurement** – reforms aimed at articulating more clearly what constitutes value in public services and how it might be measured; and

- **Mutuality** – reforms aimed at using the 'special character' of public services to change citizen and use behaviour and to help improve service delivery.

Markets, Choice and Contestability

Osborne and Gaebler's argument for the use of market mechanisms in the public realm was not a moral one about the inherent goodness of markets but a pragmatic one about their utility in creating desirable results. Like many authors before and since, they recognised that it is simply not possible for governments to control the millions of daily interactions between public-service providers and users through the design and imposition of bureaucratic programmes. As a general rule (to which there are obvious and frequently cited objections), market systems are better than administrative systems at meeting needs – and there is no reason why this general truth should apply to entertainment and not education, or to hairdressing and not healthcare (see Chapter Three in this volume by Maclean, Rossiter and Williams). The challenge for government, of course, is to create the right incentives and encourage the right behaviour. To say that market mechanisms should be used is not to imply there is no role for government. On the contrary, market design is a vital function for a government that is steering rather than rowing. This design challenge occurs on both the demand and the supply side: to ensure more and better provision for a given set of resources; and to ensure that poor people and poor communities are given the best opportunity to secure their share of the benefits that market mechanisms can bring.

There have been three significant changes to the use of

market mechanisms in the UK:

1. Structural reform - the introduction of purchaser-provider splits

2. Supply-side reform - the use of tendering and market testing to bring alternative sources of supply into public services

3. Demand-side reform – the strengthening of the power of users by, for example, improving the supply of information.

Each aspect needs to be improved and extended in turn.

(i) Structural reform - extending the purchaser-provider split
One of the Thatcher government's enduring legacies in the public realm is the purchaser-provider split. This split has created opportunities for better specification of service requirements, for the more autonomous management of operating units and for the introduction of a diverse supply-side in which in-house, commercial and not-for-profit organisations have competed for the right to deliver services. In the memorable words of Osborne & Gaebler, it allows governments to 'steer, not row', ensuring that they are not providing services which would be delivered better by other organisations.

One successful example from the 1990s was the prison service: from 1991, contracts to manage new prisons were put out to tender and, in 1993, the government decided that all new prisons would be built through the PFI. That was changed in 1998 to a process open to public and private sectors, but from 2002, the management of failing public sector prisons may be offered to the private sector. Ten out of 152 prisons in England, Scotland and Wales are managed by the private sector, and PFI now provides 6290 prison places in the private sector - directly commissioned by the Home Office. HMP Wolds was the first privately contracted prison. It was noted for its more humane regime, with prisoners referred to as "Mr" or by their first name, and staff wearing name badges. Another example of good practice involving the private sector is HMP Altcourse, a PFI prison praised for exceptional quality of regime.

There is renewed interest within government at present in the purchaser/provider model: It lies at the heart of the recently announced National Offender Management Service (NOMS), for example, reflecting the insight that skilled procurement of a package of correctional services from a diversity of sources is likely to be a better route to reducing recidivism than the route of cycling offenders through the old monopolistic prisons and probation services. Extending this model to other parts of the public sector – in particular schools and policing – could bring similar benefits:

- A purchaser-provider split in education could settle once and for all the question of what Local Education Authorities are for – the answer being to secure and help fund appropriate provision for their areas, rather than retain any residual role in management – and allow the creation of every school as an independent institution with clear accountability to its LEA for performance. Smaller and less confident schools could bundle together into consortia or federations, with aggregated management and governance structures to provide higher quality support and allow the cost advantages that come from operating at greater scale

- In policing, the clearer delineation of commissioning and delivery would reflect the successful arrangements of many US cities – notably New York. Giving the commissioning role for aspects of public-order and reassurance services to local authorities might allow some limited contestability, in which authorities might choose whether to spend more of their budget on the police (specifically, on police community support officers) or with local-authority services (such as neighbourhood or street wardens).

As in health, the introduction of a separate purchasing function creates the opportunity for greater use of differentiated funding to reflect needs and to align supply and demand more effectively – in effect, to create something more like a pricing mechanism within public services but in a way which allows those services to remain free at the point of use. In education, funding for pupils could be more sharply differentiated by pupils' background and prior attainment levels, ensuring that the more challenging and needy pupils attracted a larger budget – which would provide both a stronger incentive for schools to take such pupils and the resources to make their successful education more likely. In correctional services, market mechanisms might be used by purchasers to buy fully customised programmes of punishment and rehabilitation for individual offenders, securing these services from providers who offered the best combination of price and likelihood of a successful outcome for the individual.

(ii) Supply-side reform – increasing contestability
Properly functioning private markets are characterised by frequent changes on the supply side. This may mean new firms entering the market, successful firms increasing their capacity or less successful firms scaling back and possibly exiting the market altogether. In many markets, these changes are fuelled not by the establishment of additional capacity but by changing the organisation and ownership of the capacity that is already there – in particular, by good performers taking over less good performers.

By contrast, the supply-side for most public services has historically been tightly planned and controlled, creating a rather static – even stagnant – environment in which change is driven by bureaucratic decisions around demography and service organisation. The Government has made impressive strides to address this inflexibility in recent years with initiatives such as City Academies, star ratings for NHS trusts and a willingness to direct PCTs to use private capacity to meet health demand. But, in most parts of the public sector, it is still difficult for new providers to enter; good providers do not expand; and a poor provider can limp along for too long before a Whitehall official authorises its closure or its takeover by new management.

With an extension of the purchaser-provider split, it is possible to imagine a future in which the supply-side for public services becomes much more like that of private markets:

- The management team of a successful secondary school might look to operate at more than one site, building a small chain with a distinctive brand. Branding may relate to a specialism in a particular style or ethos of education or to a focus on children with particular needs (indeed, some non-main-streamed special education provision already follows this model). As in the private sector, chains could grow through mergers (when two schools agree to combine in the belief that their shared skills and assets will deliver better service than the sum of the parts), takeovers (when a school opens another branch on the site of a previously under-performing management team and attempts to replicate its success at the new site) and extending provision at greenfield sites (when a school helps an LEA meet its growing school-place needs by replicating itself rather than by the LEA assembling a new and untried management team to occupy the new school buildings). Such innovations would not be bound by the physical geography of any individual LEA: one could imagine, say, a branch of the London Oratory chain of schools opening up in Islington

- A social services department with an efficient and effective approach to fostering and adoption services might franchise the approach to other less successful councils. The high-performing department would contract with other councils to supply details of the operating model, help with the implementation of systems and procedures and train management and staff

- Good providers of local tax-collection and benefits administration might extend beyond their home council to deliver these services to a range of authorities, concentrating operations on a single site to create a shared service centre that could realise opportunities of scale – and continuing to add business from new authorities through marginal increases in capacity, thereby allowing the redeployment or redundancy of surplus staff from the authorities electing to contract with the successful provider.

It is possible to extend this sort of thinking into some public-service labour markets. Education is a sector in which lots of small-scale curricular and pedagogic innovations are constantly being made by highly skilled and motivated teachers. Yet the benefits of these innovations are often confined to the school in which that teacher works, or perhaps even just the classes that teacher teaches. The revolution in information and communications technology allows much of this innovation to be digitised and used at other sites, perhaps in the form of a computer-based learning package or the video-streaming of an effective lesson or lecture. Importantly, teachers can create and adapt these sorts of products themselves – and with the right sorts of infrastructure and incentives, have some control over their distribution and enjoy royalties for their use. Encouraging schools to see themselves more as purchasers of the best educational products and services – rather than as direct employers of all-purpose teachers - would allow a redesign of the teaching profession, in which some teachers would specialise in content development and delivery while others acted as selectors of material for their pupils and advisers to those pupils to help them get the best from the diverse range of materials on offer. It would also create a much more diverse and rapidly evolving set of approaches to delivering education.

The fact that these are all public-sector examples is deliberate. Of course, opening up the supply-side will bring an increased role for private and not-for-profit organisations, as has been the experience in social care. But the case for liberating talent and enterprise within the current public sector has not been made well. The best public-service management is often a lot better than the best of the private sector; indeed, this is the reason why a number of private companies active in the provision of public services have grown their pool of management talent through direct recruitment from the public sector rather than from home-grown executives who have only ever known the commercial world. Giving managers the chance to extend their reach while remaining within the harbour of the public sector – albeit in some new organisation form, such as a public-benefit corporation – would allow genuine competition and diversity between private and non-private rather than yet another wave of provider capture by 'big capital'.

The benefits of this sort of liberalisation of supply could be extensive. Organisations operating at greater scale could reduce cost and deploy skilled management across a wider base. Greater scale would provide a more secure framework within which to innovate; and the greater risk of sanctions for under-performance would encourage all suppliers to take up successful innovations more quickly (rather than waiting for them eventually to be imposed via the bureaucratic mechanism of a national inspectorate or a standards unit). Under-performance would be resolved more quickly, through the opportunity for good providers to take over the operations of less good performers. If combined with reduced prescription from central government, chaining and branding could create a more differentiated range of providers, allowing more responsiveness to different segments of service users. It is also likely that, over time, more entrepreneurial organisations would start to pay attention to marketing, advertising and the 'look and feel' of their service offerings, both to attract service users and influence their behaviour.

Realising these benefits will require regulatory reform (to permit it), the design of incentives (to encourage it), cultural change (to reinforce it) and the development of appropriate procurement mechanisms (to make it happen). The combination of regulatory change and incentive development would need to be carefully constructed, to provide successful suppliers with the freedom to manage resources and pay their management more for success while at the same time guarding against the risk of asset-stripping (for example, where one school takes over the operations of another and then siphons funding from the second school to beef up provision at its first site).

Creative thought should also be given to the purchasing mechanism. The establishment of a clear purchaser-provider split would create commissioning bodies with the remit and capacity to manage the supply side in their localities. But there is also an opportunity for service users and local communities to combine choice and voice by voting for a change in management of any of their local public services, thereby triggering a tendering process. Should they be successful in 'recalling' the management of their local school or hospital, these users might exercise further influence by lobbying their procurement body and potential suppliers to get a particular supplier to take up the challenge of managing the provision in their locality. There may even be a case for giving user and community representatives a role in approving the new suppliers. All these mechanisms would offer both a means of helping to address underperformance and at the same time an insurance policy against such underperformance arising in the first place (because incumbent suppliers would be kept on their toes).

In health, the Patient Choice initiative is not simply a means of reducing waiting times; the initiative allows a more personal and tailored contact between the NHS and patients, with the opportunity not merely to choose where an operation is to be carried out but also when.

(iii) Demand-side reform – increasing the power of users
The objective of demand-side reform can be stated simply:
to give users the maximum degree of convenience, control
and customisation that is compatible with the wider goals
of the service and with the maintenance of equity and value
for money. And there are encouraging signs of progress on
this objective:

- In health, the Patient Choice initiative is not simply a means
  of reducing waiting times; the initiative allows a more personal
  and tailored contact between the NHS and patients, with the
  opportunity not merely to choose where an operation is to be
  carried out but also when – so (as with private provision)
  patients can fit their treatment around other activities in their
  lives, rather than adjust their lives to the schedules of the NHS

- In local-authority housing, leading councils are finding ways
  to break out of the traditional, standard models of service
  provision. Camden Council's choice-based lettings scheme is
  an excellent example. In the standard British system councils
  assess the priority of applicants, put them on a waiting list,
  and assign them to council housing as it becomes available.
  In the Home Connections scheme that Camden is piloting,
  tenants use a self-assessment questionnaire to find the number
  of priority points the council will give them. Applicants view
  available properties in an "estate agent" or on the web, and
  bid for them online or over the phone using their priority points
  score. The highest priority bidder wins, views the property, and
  moves in. Because successful bids are published applicants
  can see their chances of success. There are savings because
  fewer properties lie vacant. Applicants have more choice over
  where they live, within and across borough boundaries.
  Applicants are able to balance location, size and waiting time
  according to their own preference, not that of the council.
  Since starting in 2002 there have been over 30,000 "bids" and
  more than 650 homes have been let. In effect, the council has
  reinvented its role, and set itself up as the 'purchaser' – in this
  case by creating a system that enables the citizen to choose
  effectively between a range of providers.

This model of choice bringing convenience and control is a
powerful and attractive one. There may be scope to extend it to
other services. Given the variations in demand, capacity and
efficiency in benefits processing between local-authority providers,

it might be possible to establish some sort of guarantee of applications being processed and decisions being made within a certain time; if a local authority's current provider was unable to meet this deadline, it would be required to hand over the case (and an appropriate amount of money) to another provider.

The other aspect of user empowerment is customisation. Just as in many private markets, users now expect to be able to 'have it their way' rather than receiving a standard, uniform service that does not meet their needs. Again, there are examples of good practice in health and social care, with more tailored packages of service organised around the formal assessment of an individual's needs. The introduction of NOMS allows this sort of thinking to infuse correctional services.

Arguably, the service in which most can be done to extend customisation is school education, where – despite all the evidence from educational psychology about different learning styles – there are strong institutional and system-wide pressures to serve up standard fare, whether it appeals or not. With the introduction of greater flexibility and diversity on the supply side of education, it should be possible to devise and deliver a much more customised Programme of Learning for each pupil from the start of Key Stage 4 (and possibly from the start of secondary school), taking account of what each pupil likes and is good at, and identifying barriers to learning within the pupil's life. The customised programme would involve purchasing a more flexible set of educational experiences – some at the school and others off-site, some delivered in whole-class format and others in smaller groups or using computer-based learning – and allowing the pupil to take tests and exams when she/he is ready (as is currently the case in the assessment of, say, musical achievement), reflecting the fact that different pupils learn at different rates.

In effect, schools of the future could become 'clearing houses' helping structure, order and monitor the delivery of a package of learning and development services to pupils from a wide range of providers, some of which may be in-house, others of which may be from tutoring companies, health clubs, sports centres, local firms providing work experience, and local colleges sharing learning facilities. Within such a structure, a school governing body could take the 'intelligent purchaser' role if effectively resourced, able to buy in school management and teaching delivery services from professionals together with capacity at a range of other educational and training facilities (colleges, other schools, sports centres, local companies, local specialist tuition providers) to supplement core curriculum delivery. This will require action on a number of fronts:

• Increasing contestability and decreasing prescription on the supply side, to create a greater diversity of offerings between which users can choose

• Improving the flow of information – about what is available where and about what is good. This is partly a matter of getting better systems to allow the alignment of supply and demand across a service (as is being developed for health via the Patient Choice initiative) but also a matter of getting and interpreting data on performance

• Providing support to individual users – through designating public-service providers (such as GPs and certain teachers) as intermediaries, agents and brokers with the responsibility to assist users in making informed choices, and through an ongoing process of educating people in how to become better users of public services

• Providing users with effective power to exercise choice – through enshrining the right under certain circumstances for access to an alternative supplier (again, following the emerging model in health)

• More controversially, revisiting the vexed question of whether to offer users direct control through some form of voucher system. Throughout the 1980s and 1990s, vouchers have been viewed as anathema by virtually all of the left and much of the right. Reforms to the supply-side, such as those envisaged above, that create greater diversity and allow a more rapid expansion of capacity, may make vouchers simultaneously more acceptable and less necessary. It may be that the answer lies in the very focused use of vouchers alongside other techniques: for example, the government might wish to equalise some of the advantage that better-off parents purchase for their children via private coaching and tuition (whether to extend their child's strengths or ameliorate their weaknesses) by providing all parents of secondary-age pupils with a voucher for the purchase of some such services from accredited suppliers.

Management

Osborne and Gaebler observed that governments have a much greater appetite for designing programmes than for designing markets. If it is accepted that markets are a better means of influencing behaviour than programmes, it follows that governments should be running fewer top-down programmes to cut costs and raise performance, leaving these sorts of improvements to the managers of individual operating units working within the highly effective market mechanisms that governments have structured. Those markets should create a self-sustaining dynamic for improvement, in which pressure from rivals and from users would mean that each supplier would be looking for successful innovations and good practices that they could copy and adapt.

The proper locus of managerial effort and improvement then becomes the individual organisation or operating unit, not the whole service at a national level. And the right answer to the challenge of modernising management is for government as far as possible to stay out of the process, scaling back its efforts to produce service-wide strategies, plans, targets and performance-management regimes.

The challenge with this line of argument is recognising when to depart from it on the grounds that a) it is a statement of an ideal that, in practice, does not currently apply in any public service, and b) many of these services currently face problems that might be improved right now by top-down initiatives. Too many departures will mean that government remains stuck in its programme mindset and never gets round to solving the problems properly by structuring the right set of market mechanisms. Too few departures mean that improvement opportunities go begging in the short-term – perhaps with disastrous electoral consequences.

It is worth dwelling a moment on two examples which may be temporary exceptions to the desire to eliminate national programmes: (i) information technology (IT) and (ii) personnel.

(i) Information Technology
Reinventing Government was published in 1992: the same year as *Reengineering the Corporation* and the associated business process reengineering movement. This was several years in

advance of most people's exposure to the internet and the accompanying revolution in information and communications technology. Much of the changes to private sector management since has been informed by these two processes: redrawing the boundaries of corporations, unbundling large bureaucratic entities and designing new strategies for sourcing and collaboration. Functions that were once considered to require direct management within an organisation – such as finance, human resources and procurement – are now often outsourced to specialist suppliers working in different continents. Much customer contact has shifted from face-to-face interaction to telephone or internet-based channels. And technology has been used to redesign many business and operational models in ways that would have been hard to imagine at the start of the 1990s.

Such observations have been made so often that they have become clichés. Regrettably, it is also a cliché to observe that comparatively little progress has been made on these issues in the UK public sector, where many of the models for organising and delivering services have remained largely unchanged over the last decade. The government has taken encouraging steps to address these deficiencies recently: to take two examples, the Gershon Efficiency Review and the NHS IT modernisation programme both have the potential to create beneficial change on a large scale, cutting costs and improving quality.

It will be interesting to see whether the cautious radicalism of the Efficiency Review's early thinking is adopted across government as the means to achieve the challenging financial and performance targets set in the 2004 Spending Review. In particular, departments may consider the merits of securing cost savings and quality improvements in the back-office functions of finance, Human Resources and procurement through aggregation and new sourcing strategies (whether to private suppliers or to a smaller number of high-performing public-sector providers with a readiness to shift operations away from expensive locations in London – even possibly off-shore). And, assuming that the initial momentum of the NHS IT programme is maintained through to successful execution, there may be scope to extend the successes of this approach to other public services where investment in IT and process redesign has been slower (for example, policing and the criminal justice system) –

perhaps driven from the centre of government if departments fail to respond to the challenge.

IT and process-driven change will also be aided by a willingness on the part of the Government to move away from crude measures of staff numbers as a proxy for levels of service and from the central prescription of single models of service delivery. In policing, the continuing willingness of both main parties to demonstrate their political virility with reference to the number of holders of the office of constable is particularly depressing, especially when so much officer time is not spent on operational or visible policing. A focus on outcomes, with police authorities and senior managers given freedom to spend money on any combination of staff (whether sworn constables, other policing operatives or civil support workers), technology and equipment in furtherance of those outcomes, would be more likely to stimulate innovation in service redesign and improvement.

Such innovation would be further served by the creation of investment pots – whether from public or private sources – to fund pilots of new delivery models: for example, in schools, where considerable scope exists to design an approach that moves away from single teachers using 'chalk and talk' methods to a plurality of technologies and learning environments (including lessons in neighbouring schools as well as more work- and home-based learning) to reflect pupils' interests, aptitudes and learning styles and to ensure each pupil gets the best possible access to effective instruction. Some schools (for example, Highdown School in Reading) have started to embrace such alternative models. Seed funding could help spread this sort of innovation; though care should be taken by government to use such interventions sparingly if it is not to fall back into the top-down programme mindset, thereby crowding out the space for market mechanisms to stimulate decentralised organisations to develop their own solutions.

(ii) Personnel
The last decade has also seen significant change in another set of issues on which Osborne and Gaebler were largely silent: patterns of employment and remuneration. In the private sector, these changes have taken place at the level of the workforce and

of senior management. Greater flexibility in employment has been used to get a better fit between companies' capacity and demand, and also to allow the removal of poor performers. As a corollary, most companies have been obsessed about ways in which remuneration packages can be tweaked to create the best set of incentives for good performance at all levels, but especially among senior management.

Much private-sector practice in these respects is not to be commended. But the underlying principles – that good performance should be rewarded handsomely (to get and keep star performers) and that it should be easy and near-obligatory to remove poor performers at each and every level – might be applied more vigorously to the public sector than they are at present. Osborne and Gaebler's paradigm assumes that public services will enjoy access to a steady supply of motivated and talented managers and that their reward would arise largely from the satisfaction of good work in the public service. But wouldn't the pool of candidates increase if salaries for senior management positions were to rise significantly? For example, successful leaders of secondary schools (or school consortia) could look to earn as the norm, say, £150,000 or more; and successful top civil-servants and heads of urban police forces, say, £300,000 or more. Such salaries would need to be accompanied by tight performance-management arrangements to allow the removal of poor performers; but this raising of risks and rewards would give more appropriate compensation for the highly demanding roles that exist at the top of public-service organisations.

These changes could be aligned with further reforms to widen the pool of potential candidates for top-management positions by removing any remaining barriers to non-professionals leading public services. While it is now commonplace for hospital trusts to be run by managers who are not clinicians, it is still not possible for any police force other than the Met (which, in passing, had as its first commissioner one Robert Peel - a non-policing professional who was nevertheless able to devise and execute a model of policing by consent that is still relevant 175 years later) to be headed by someone who is not a member of the Association of Chief Police Officers. It is very rare for any school or federation of schools to be run by a non-teacher. Yet the experience from many organisations and sectors is that executives not steeped in that organisation's or sector's culture can be a highly effective way of introducing innovation, challenging conventional wisdom and enabling lasting cultural change. If we want our police forces and schools to be different, we may want to think about having at least a few people at the top of them who will not be inclined to carry on doing what those organisations have always done. Such changes would reinforce the growing – and healthy – trend for talented managers to move between public and private sectors, creating a dynamic that benefits both sectors.

These principles can be applied throughout the public sector. Good staff at all levels should be rewarded more effectively for their work; and it should be easier to remove poor performers. Too many public services remain clogged with staff who lack the motivation or ability to perform well; but it remains extremely difficult to remove poorly performing civil servants or police officers. Again the extremes of some private-sector practice – for example, the approach adopted historically by GE in which the bottom 5% of performers was dismissed each year – might be inappropriate. But the introduction of standard five or seven-year fixed term contracts in the civil service and the police, in which under-performers might not be offered a follow-on contract, would be an effective way of ensuring that organisations were not weighed down by the need to find spaces for employees who had ceased to be able to meet the demands of the service.

Public Value

I said above that the vision of Osborne and Gaebler needed to be supplemented, to address their lack of thinking on models of value. *Reinventing Government* placed great emphasis on the importance of performance measurement, going so far as to dedicate an appendix to the 'art' of measuring the right things in the right ways. Osborne and Gaebler recognized the vital role that performance measures play in informing users and potential users about an organisation's performance, and helping users and citizens to exercise both choice and voice. But they were not explicit about the underlying purpose of performance measurement within any organisation – namely, the alignment

1 Moore, Mark, *Creating Public Value*, 1995.

of efforts towards the creation of value by that organisation. Certainly, success in public-service delivery – and therefore, given the rising relative importance of public services in 21st century politics, success in politics more broadly - will come down to perceptions of value. Citizens need to be convinced that what they value about public services is improving; and they also need to be satisfied that the taxes and charges they pay for these services represent value for money.

So, when formulating and executing its strategy for public-service reform, the government needs mechanisms that focus both politicians and managers on these questions of value. What it currently uses is still very much out of *Reinventing Government's* appendix: lots of measures and targets, without an explicit model of value underpinning them. Sadly, a number of the errors listed by Osborne and Gaebler – a bias towards inputs and outputs rather than outcomes, too many measures and too many targets, top-down imposition of measures (creating resistance, destroying morale and encouraging cheating), and the risk of perverse incentives – are still being made. And, perhaps more tellingly, the current approach to measurement and target-setting leaves the Government with: insufficient focus on citizens and their requirements; an inability to identify and act upon the drivers of value; and a difficulty for politicians in acting as effective overseers and communicators of progress in service delivery.

This last point is particularly important. Politicians can be lulled into a false sense of security by progress against targets – but when they try to lull the public into a similar sense by reeling off statistics, the public will be unimpressed unless what they experience in their locality and from their local school, hospital or police service accords with the political message. And even if these service experiences are positive, the current performance-measurement regime does not help politicians focus on the key trade-off on which they will be judged: the extent to which any improvement in service delivery comes with a level of cost-effectiveness that allows a reasonable 'price' to be paid in terms of taxes and charges.

(i) Models of Public Value

Mark Moore's work on public value[1] and more recent papers in the UK[2] have laid some of the foundations for a model of public value that could help address these challenges. The strengths of this published work is in the consensus it has started to fashion around public value being a bundle of desired outcomes that - with varying applicability and significance - combine user satisfaction, wider social benefits (whether in the form of fulfilling a service's statutory duties or in the form of meeting wider public expectations of that service), the building of trust in public institutions, and the achievement of economy and efficiency in delivering these benefits.

Recent work by Accenture on the creation of its Public Sector Value (PSV) model[3] has attempted to build on the foundations laid by Moore *et al* and address the outstanding challenges by adapting the model of Shareholder Value Analysis (SVA), which is widely accepted among academic and commercial opinion (both among executives and the investment community) as the best way to assess a company's performance and make key strategic choices on issues such as mergers and acquisitions. Overall, the clarity of the SVA model (and the ability to capture it through overarching measures of performance to which more detailed operational measures and targets are subordinate) allows managers in successful companies to focus on what is most important – satisfying customers in a way that generates profitable growth in order to maximise value for shareholders - and to be held to account by those shareholders, to whom they are ultimately responsible.

There are inherent difficulties with applying private-sector models of value to the public sector. Government departments and agencies do not have shareholders, shares or markets in which those shares can be bought and sold and hence priced. Government services do not exist to generate and maximise profits. Comparisons within and between parts of the public sector are difficult; and even if they were not, politicians are rarely as willing and able as commercial investors to be discriminating in their choices about where to place their money according to the expected return. One citizen can differ dramatically from another in what he or she values from a public service; and, indeed, citizens' perceptions of value may change over time – according to, for example, whether they make more or less use of a public service. In addition, the

2 Kelly, Gavin, & Muers, Stephen, *Creating Public Value: a new framework for public – sector reform*, Cabinet Office 2003. Chapman, Jake, 'Public Value: the missing ingredient in reform?' in *The Adaptive State*, Demos 2003.

3 A US patent is pending for the Accenture Public Sector Value model. For further information on the model, contact greg.wilkinson@accenture.com.

application of private sector models to the public or not-for-profit sector risks meeting with cultural resistance.

Despite these difficulties, there may be opportunities that could flow from adapting the key underlying principles of the SVA model. The Accenture model of PSV:

- identifies the citizen as the stakeholder whose interests should be accorded primacy

- posits, for each service or organisation, the principal factors that constitute value for citizens, using 80/20 thinking to identify the small number of factors (normally no more than about half a dozen) that really drive citizens' overall assessment of that service

- tracks these components of value via a small number of quantitative measures – specially, a single score for outcomes (combining user satisfaction, public confidence and the fulfilment of statutory duties and wider public expectations) and a single score for cost-effectiveness (the weighted outcome measure divided by a measure of the financial resources that are being consumed to deliver those outcomes)

- plots outcomes against cost-effectiveness to understand trends in an organisation's performance over time, with particular attention paid to the interplay between outcomes and cost-effectiveness to assess whether good performance in one dimension is being achieved at the expense of performance in the other

- allows comparisons to be made between similar organisations in the same sector (and, with appropriate adjustments, between similar services in different countries) and allows the drivers of value to be identified from closer assessment of high-performing public-service organisations.

(ii) Public value - benefits and limitations

Such a model of value could supplement a much smaller set of standards and targets (which would be focused on issues of access to services), creating a streamlined set of measures to replace the current plethora of requirements arising from PSAs and assorted national plans and strategies. They would represent a move away from the UK's current centralised performance-management regimes in which central agents prescribe many targets that operational managers must meet, and replace it with a more decentralised approach in which the centre develops a smaller number of measures – around access and value - against which managers should maximize performance. The top-down approach, fashionable for large parts of the late twentieth century, has now largely been abandoned by forward-looking and successful organisations; and it is time for it to be replaced in the public sector. A new, value-based approach could have four distinct advantages. It could:

(a) Enable a focus on the citizen in service organisation and delivery
Models of value require politicians, officials and executives to identify the priority outcomes citizens require from a public service and to ensure that these are pursued cost-effectively. By placing the citizen's interests at the heart of the measurement process, it is likely that managers and staff will be more effectively focused on meeting those needs when delivering services.

(b) Encourage a move from target-meeting to value-maximis-ing behaviour
One of the difficulties of managing within a framework of targets is reconciling Tom Peters' insight that 'the man who has 25 priorities has none' with the constant temptation to add just one more objective or target to an organisation's agenda. Operational managers find it difficult to perform when given too many targets; they also find it difficult to resist adjusting their mindset from a belief in doing the best job they can to simply doing enough to meet the target. As a consequence, a measurement system based on meeting targets is likely to be sub-optimal by comparison with a system that operated with only a small number of value-based measures and required managers to maximise performance against these measures.

(c) Promote understanding of how to maximise value
The use of valuation techniques in the private-sector shows that it is possible to move very quickly from an evaluation of how well a company is doing to understanding why its performance is as it is and what can be done to improve it. The power of val-uation measures is that they encourage and allow analysts and managers to move quickly to the identification of value drivers.

4 *The Measurement Malaise,*
The Economist 2002.

Operational managers find it difficult to perform when given too many targets; they also find it difficult to resist adjusting their mindset from a belief in doing the best job they can to simply doing enough to meet the target.

There is a hunger to learn what it is that enables industry leaders to succeed. Any system of measurement that shifted the debate from whether a desired outcome had been met (and from the belief that simply setting operational managers a target – with the nebulous threat of some form of top-down pressure in the event of under-performance - is sufficient to achieve it) to an understanding of how managers could improve performance is of great potential benefit.

(d) Strengthen accountability
One criticism of the multiplicity of current Government targets is the extent to which public sector managers can be seen to avoid clear accountability for failing in some areas by succeeding in others.[4] By providing an approximation of the actual value delivered to citizens, a public value perspective combines multiple outcomes and a consideration of resources to present a pared-down 'citizen focused' assessment of a public organisation's performance – increasing accountability to the public and to government.

Sceptical academics and harassed public-service managers will raise – understandably - a number of questions about such a model. Two points should be acknowledged:

- public value scores will mean different things in different industries. As a consequence, the methodology will not place public-sector decision-makers in the position of private investors – who have the ability to consider the merits of investing in a pharmaceutical company or a retailer with reference to the common currency of the financial return they will get from each option. Again, it is important to remember that this is a problem with any system of performance measurement in the public sector – and it is one of the reasons why there is an irreducible role for political judgement in decision-making about the use of public resources

- the devil is in the detail. The model relies on a process of boiling down a multiplicity of objectives into a small number of measures for inclusion within a basket of outcomes; and it also requires the weighting of those outcomes, and of financial performance, to create aggregate measures. These steps are laden with assumptions; and it is likely that at least some stakeholders will disagree with some of those assumptions. As a consequence the approach is always likely to be on shakier ground than the SVA approach used in the private sector. But we should not shy away from trying to create summary assessments that aggregate and combine apparently incommensurable aspects of performance, not least because this process of aggregation is exactly what managers, politicians and citizens do when they take their respective decisions on operational priorities, the allocation of resources and whether to vote for the incumbent administration or replace them with a rival set of politicians that offer the prospect of better public value for taxpayers' money. And, without some attempt to translate these summary assessments into quantitative form, it will not be possible to move beyond the rather woolly discussions of public value that – to date – have proved to be of interest but of little practical use.

Measurement matters. The wrong sort of system demotivates and demoralises managers and staff and can lead to an incorrect focus of resources and effort. The right system of measurement can improve the way in which services are managed and delivered, thereby help bring about a transformation in citizens' experience of those services. Evolving the UK's measurement system to one more explicitly underpinned by a conception of public value would be a powerful means of reinforcing the other components of the next stage of public-service reform.

Mutuality, Public Engagement and Personal Responsibility
Critics of the approach set out in this essay have argued that Osborne and Gaebler's work – and, more generally, the language of markets and management – obscures a vital aspect of

the public realm. For these critics, the relationships between the state, the public-service employee, the service user and the citizen have a 'special' character; in these relationships, there is more than a simple transaction taking place between a service provider and a passive consumer – we all approach public services as members of a polity, with provider employees motivated by a public service ethos and users by their additional role as citizens. This line of argument is only partially correct, for the following reasons:

- Its first implication is that relationships in private markets are purely instrumental. Yet many businesses agonise over how to build and maintain a special relationship with their employees in which people turn up to work with their hearts as well as their brains and hands, and look for ways to reinforce employee loyalty and motivation – for example, by creating a degree of employee ownership. And most service businesses attempt to shape and influence the behaviour of their customers to allow more efficient and effective delivery: some use branding and direct communication to create a sense of belonging to a 'club' involving both company and customer; others go as far as to give their customers stakes in the business. (Indeed, it is an irony that many of these ideas were developed from within the rich socialist tradition of the co-operative movement)

- Its second implication is that relationships based on instrumental calculations of utility and relationships based on trust and the establishment of social capital are mutually exclusive. This is not the case in many private markets. It is unclear why it should be the case in the provision of public services such as education, health and policing.

But there is merit in the argument that reciprocity, mutuality, engagement and personal responsibility may provide a rich vein of possibilities for improving the delivery of public services. Seeing citizens and users as active agents rather than passive recipients, from whom something other than consumption is required if public services are to be effective, may help tackle some of the deep-rooted problems around education, health and public-order outcomes that have proved frustratingly persistent despite well over ten years of reforms to the provider side of the equation. This insight is particularly relevant to those of us on the left, who see public services as playing a role in the redistribution of advantage and the creation of a fairer, more equal society. Advantage is certainly aided by access to financial assets; but its real foundations lie in factors such as safety and security, self-confidence and self-esteem, knowledge, culture, relationships and physical and psychological health – and these are only partly determined by money. Certainly, the evidence of the second half of the twentieth century is that they are influenced less by transfer payments and paternalistically delivered welfare services, and more by changing people's behaviour and lifestyle choices. Changing behaviour requires a different set of skills and techniques – and it may be that the principle of mutuality can help achieve these goals.

Mutuality In Practice

There are a number of examples of mutuality in public services, in the UK and elsewhere:

- Policing in a number of American cities has been transformed by the introduction of reassurance-based operations, in which officers get out of reactive, car-based work (driving around areas at high speed responding to 911 calls) and back into foot-based beat work, with priorities informed and driven by regular meetings with the local community at which residents highlight issues of concern. The process is reciprocal: in return for attending the meetings, the citizens see their concerns addressed; in return for becoming more user-focused, the police receive valuable community intelligence that helps bring offenders to justice. One of the most successful examples of this style of working has been in Chicago, where the Chicago Alternative Policing Strategy has helped the city achieve reductions of 18 % in murder, 19 % in theft, 31 % in robbery and 37 % in burglary over the period of 1996 – 2002

Education in cities such as Birmingham has been strengthened by the success of home-school contracts, by new models of pre-school and primary-school services that engage parents far more.

• Education in cities such as Birmingham has been strengthened by the success of home-school contracts, by new models of pre-school and primary-school services that engage parents far more, and by the development of stronger relationships between schools and other community assets such as football clubs and community centres, at which space can be made for out-of-school learning supported by the school.

• Health outcomes are starting to be favourably impacted across the UK by the work of the 350 Healthy Living Centres (HLCs) set up by the Big Lottery Fund to pursue alternative, community-based approaches to health promotion. Working with a more explicitly social model of health (which recognises the interplay between economic and social outcomes in a community and which understands the limitations of clinician-run approaches to public health) and often managed by social enterprises and voluntary organisations with strong roots in their local communities, HLCs fund and run clubs, networks and community businesses covering everything from meditation classes to community gardening.

• Leading local authorities are starting to engage more extensively with their communities when formulating strategy. Kirklees Metropolitan Borough Council is developing new styles of working to improve its focus on service improvement. It has a broad range of mechanisms in place: targeted consultation exercises, a citizens' panel, numerous networks and community groups, and local area committees. The council has a good awareness of national and local priorities and uses this to influence corporate priorities and service strategy. Examples of good practice include: a community strategy based on extensive consultation with community and voluntary groups, the public, other public sector organisations and the private sector, which has enabled the LSP to identify key local issues; revised approaches to reporting repairs and allocations, good relations with tenants' groups through regular work with them to monitor the conditions of estates and implement local estate improvements, as well as housing policy and practice; extensive consultation in regeneration areas to shape local programmes; and; working with community leaders to identify and respond to the priorities of minority ethnic communities within these areas. The outcome of this approach is Kirklees' Vision 2012 Community Strategy – setting the agenda for service improvements in its neighbourhood

renewal strategybased on consultation with users, partners
and stakeholders.

It is possible to imagine going further and faster with each of
these types of initiative. Schools could invest more of their time
in relationships with parents – not just through traditional
channels such as the parents' evening and the periodic meetings
between parents and governors, but also through email and
web-based access – or even through home visits. GPs could
work alongside HLCs to help fund, establish and advise self-
managed exercise clubs. Policing in large urban areas could
be transformed by deploying in every ward a small team of
named officers who were the designated guardians for that
area, contactable via a direct line (with the names of the officers
and their telephone numbers posted to every dwelling in the
ward) and with an explicit remit to build personal relationships
with citizens in their locality.

More broadly, the principle of mutuality could be extended
into local governance. The establishment of neighbourhood
councils in urban areas, on which elected representatives could
spend no more than a few hours each week taking responsibility
for a proportion of expenditure on environmental services
(roads, street cleaning, parks, play areas etc) across areas
spanning no more than a few wards, could bring into public
service a new stratum of people with a remit of engaging
local communities and changing behaviour. These goals may
be achievable at the micro-level – which allows almost a
'commune' mentality of self-management, and the co-production
of services around the local environment - in a way that has
rarely proved possible within traditional borough and district
local government structures, with their endless meetings and
separation from community life.

Mutuality: Recommendations For Action
Mutuality is a fuzzy concept. This fuzziness may be one of
the reasons why it has not yet received the attention it deserves
as a tool for reforming public services: it does not lend itself
to central regulation or political diktat. (Indeed, the best way
of killing the idea would be to require every public-service
provider to draw up a Mutuality Strategy, with targets monitored

by a unit in the Cabinet Office.) As a consequence, it is hard to draw up concrete recommendations for action. But there are steps that government can take to encourage innovation around the theme of mutuality:

- Politicians can change the language of debate around public-services reform, arguing for the development of mutual solutions as a key part of the direction they wish reform to take and championing good examples of this style of working. But language will not be enough. A shift towards mutuality will involve a significant change to the culture of public-services reform: and, like any change in culture, it will succeed only if the intentions and behaviour of government changes along with its new words. If mutuality is not anchored in a mindset based on mutual respect, and if it is treated as yet another opportunity for politicians to wield power and authority (whether in an authoritarian way or just simply in a paternalistic and patronising way) over the poor and the disadvantaged, then – like all other similar attempts to solve complex problems with crude mechanisms – it will be seen as spin and a sham, and will be doomed to failure

- Government can channel funding towards initiatives that support mutuality. It can create forms of governance that reinforce it – such as neighbourhood councils. And it can remove initiatives from previous waves of reform that obstruct the development of mutuality – for example, the focus on police numbers (rather than on how the police actually spend their time) and the direction of policing activity towards nationally-set priorities that crowd out space for local solutions

---

Schools could invest more of their time in relationships with parents – not just through traditional channels such as the parents' evening and the periodic meetings between parents and governors, but also through email and web-based access – or even through home visits.

- Crucially, governments can design and establish market mechanisms – because the threat of removal from competition is perhaps the best way of encouraging providers to build the close and effective relationships with their users that lie at the heart of any mutual solution. Indeed, in the private sector such relationships are often highly effective at entrenching a firm's market position and creating barriers to entry.

Targeting The New Programme Of Reform

On their own, none of the issues explored above – creating markets, encouraging and enabling a more sophisticated approach to management, developing mutuality in service design and delivery, and formulating a clearer understanding of what constitutes value in each public service (and how to measure it) – will be sufficient to ensure radical reform of any public service. The reformer's skill is in combining these techniques. The desired results can be stated in a straightforward way: building the motivation and releasing the energy of current and potential purchasers and suppliers; ensuring that there is sufficient direction while avoiding the risk of micro-management; and creating the right set of incentives, rewards and sanctions while taking care to nurture the public service ethos that drives many staff.

How to mix and blend reforms to achieve these results is less easily prescribed. All services would benefit from greater clarity around value and its measurement, and from a consequent scaling back of measures and targets. And it is only fair that management and staff in all services should be offered more significant rewards for success, to balance the greater insecurity that fundamental reform will bring. Beyond these common features, a high-level outline prescription for each service might go as follows:

- For *policing*, the limited scope for contestability and competition and the current shortcomings in many of the enablers of effective performance (for example, the coherence of current organisational structures, the strength and clarity of current accountability mechanisms, the adequacy of existing IT, the barriers created by current personnel regulations, the limited understanding and dissemination of good practice across the service, the lack of diversity of senior management and the difficulties in embedding cultural change within forces) may create a continuing need for a top-down programme of Government-directed change to address these shortcomings for any but the largest of forces. But there is much that all forces can do to develop approaches rooted in mutuality – particularly in relation to community engagement

• For *education*, the structural reform of a purchaser-provider split would be a powerful starting point. The combination of regulations and incentives to stimulate greater contestability, along with a relaxation of national direction (at least in the secondary sector) in relation to both curriculum and pedagogy would open up the possibility of a much more vibrant and diverse supply side – with good providers expanding and less good providers closing more quickly. This possibility (irrespective of how much it happens in practice) should be sufficient to stimulate higher performance across the sector. Less prescription would also allow innovation in service design and delivery – a process that would be supported by enabling the intellectual property of individual teachers to be traded more freely between schools. To get the most from this increasing diversity, pupils and parents should be offered access to learning mentors and advisers who would help the pupil assemble a personalised learning plan; and there may be some merit in limited use of a voucher mechanism to allow parents to purchase extra coaching and tuition services out of school time from accredited suppliers. It is likely that the desire of most heads and teachers to respond to the mutuality agenda will be stimulated – not restricted – by the introduction of market mechanisms, since the development of strong mutual relations between schools and parents will be one of the most effective defences against closure by the purchasing LEA or takeover by a more successful chain of schools

• For *health,* as high levels of investment continue to bring improved standards of access and clinical quality, the challenge will be to improve the workings of the purchaser-provider relationship to identify and correct mismatches between supply and demand. Getting the money to follow the patient, and extending reforms such as Patient Choice, are helpful enablers of this change. But more needs to be done to inform individual choice: in particular, getting and acting on more data on variations

in quality between individual facilities and teams of staff
(particularly clinicians), and ensuring a stronger agent-intermediary
role for GPs and PCT-social services assessment staff in
helping broker the best package of medical and social care for
individuals. And, beyond more rapid access and better acute
facilities, the real breakthroughs in health outcomes are likely
to come from finding ways in people can change behaviour
and lifestyles. Ideas of mutuality are likely to be vital. Success
will involve finding techniques and organisations that can
overcome the complex social and psychological barriers
to personal change. And it may be that, learning from the
experience to date of the best Healthy Living Centres, a different
sort of market – between social entrepreneurs and voluntary
organisations with the credibility and ability to get people with
unhealthy lifestyles to change – is required to achieve this sort
of success

- For *Whitehall*, the challenge will be to allow the stimuli of
market forces and mutuality within decentralised systems to
generate more sophisticated management of individual operating
units, ensuring wherever possible that these improvements
are bottom-up rather than top-down, and (with the possible
exception of policing) scaling back attempts to manage
performance via national initiatives and regimes. The correct
role for central government is not to attempt to manage
whole-service performance via plans, targets and initiatives,
but rather to define value in services for which accountability
lies at the national level; provide funding for services, again
reflecting the agreed division of responsibility between

---

*The correct role for central government
is not to attempt to manage whole-service
performance via plans, targets and
initiatives, but rather to define value
in services for which accountability
lies at the national level.*

---

central and local government; and construct appropriate
market mechanisms for each service that allow the
creation of self-sustaining systems

- Such an approach does not mean the end of the
much-criticised functions of *audit and inspection*; in the
proposed public-service markets, these functions will have
a role in providing reliable data to help inform the decisions
of users, purchasers, operational managers and politicians.
They can also play a role in helping to identify good practice
(a function that should be unnecessary if markets work well,
but one for which there is likely to be a need and demand for
some years to come). But these more limited roles, along with
a scaling back of the panoply of performance measures and
targets, should mean the high-water mark of audit and
inspection in the UK has been reached.

Conclusion

Mario Cuomo once observed that politicians campaign in
poetry and govern in prose. Few would dispute that the language
and concepts of 'reinventing government' are irretrievably
prosaic. But it is important to remember that the challenge
outlined in this chapter is a fundamentally political one, in two
respects. The first is that reinvention offers a series of tools and
techniques that leave the key questions of political strategy –
what do we want, for whom, and with what goals in mind –
unanswered; answers to these political questions, providing
a clear sense of purpose and direction about the sort of society
government is trying to help create, will be essential. The
second is that the development and implementation of a new
wave of reinvention is likely to face active and passive resistance
from a number of sources; political capital will need to be
expended in overcoming these obstacles. Politicians need to
make a judgement about whether the rewards of reinvention
are worth the effort.

   For the current government, reinvention offers two
potential sets of rewards. The first is that the sorts of mechanisms
outlined in this chapter provide the opportunity to reach the
disadvantaged, the poor and the excluded in ways that go
beyond what the government has achieved to date. The second
is that they open up the possibility of higher levels of service

that offer more choice, convenience and control for more people. If those services are to be good enough to help create a fairer and more just society, bureaucratic and managerial tinkering will not be enough. Real reinvention will be required; and this task is too important to be left to the technocrats. It will also require politics.